Hey,

DEMCO

Other Books by Leland Gregory

What's the Number for 911?
What's the Number for 911 Again?
The Stupid Crook Book

Hey, Idiot!

Chronicles of Human Stupidity

- - - - -

Leland Gregory

- - - - -

**Andrews McMeel
Publishing**

Kansas City

Hey, Idiot!

04 05 06 07 FFG 10 9 8 7 6 5 4 3

Library of Congress Cataloging-in-Publication Data

Gregory, Leland
    Hey idiot! : chronicles of human stupidity / Leland Gregory.
      p. cm.
    ISBN 0-7407-3902-6
    1. Stupidity—Anecdotes. I. Title.

BF431.G7825 2003
081—dc21

2003052448

Attention: Schools and Businesses

This book is dedicated to my beautiful wife,
Gloria G. Gregory, who has given me everything
I could ever wish for, including our son, Nicholas.
We live in strange times and there's no one
who helps me laugh about it more than you, Glo.

Contents

Idiotic Excuses

Shooting Blanks

A scientist in Atlanta collected more than ten pounds of bullet shell casings from the city's streets during lunch hours. The casings ranged from .22 caliber to bullets used in the AK-47 assault rifle. Commenting on the scientist's collection, police officials in Atlanta said that didn't necessarily mean the city isn't safe. Their theory was that people could be firing their weapons elsewhere and leaving the shells in Atlanta. Now, that's a long shot.

———————————

Sometimes when I'm sleeping, you know, it's like, in the middle of the night I'm not, like, totally clear. I'm thinking I'm sleeping with my wife. . . . I'm not even attracted to you! I am 150 to 200 percent happy with the wife that I have.

—Survivor: Thailand *castaway Ted Rogers, Jr., apologizing to tribemate Ghadnia Johnson, after she accused him of "grinding" against her in her sleep*

A Cheeky Fellow

Known mobster Vincent "Gigi Portalla" Marino has complained for years that federal agents planted something on him during surgery to remove a bullet from his buttocks. Marino was granted a hearing to reveal the truth and the region's top federal law enforcement official denied his account—that federal agents put a tracking devise in his butt. "We can confirm that the U.S. Drug Enforcement Administration did not implant a tracking device in defendant Vincent M. 'Gigi Portalla' Marino's buttocks," U.S. Attorney Donald Stern said in a statement. "But we cannot speak, however, for any extra-terrestrial beings." U.S. District Judge Nathaniel Gorton said the situation "sounds like some DEA agent trying to be funny," but he honored Marino's request to force the government to tell him the truth about the device. Maybe that's where the expression "having a bug up your butt" came from.

A man who had just robbed a branch of the U.S. Bank in Sacramento, California, explained his actions to a bank employee: **"I only wanted to teach you a lesson. I want a job in bank security."** The man's claims would have had more merit had he not been previously convicted of five bank robberies with another bank robbery conviction pending.

Hey, Idiot!

I'm Checking on It

An assistant professor of art history at Northwestern University in Evanston, Illinois, collected $33,000 in Social Security checks for his mother before finally notifying the government that his mother had died. He had allowed the checks to be electronically deposited into the joint account he shared with his mother for five years without telling anyone of her passing. The professor's lawyer described his client's actions as "extreme procrastination behavior" brought on by depression following the death of his mother. I'll bet the professor has at least thirty-three thousand reasons for not reporting his mother's death to Social Security officials.

— — — — — — — — —

I do touch too much bread, yes,
more than the next person.

—Samuel Feldman, convicted of fondling $1,000 worth
of baked goods in Philadelphia stores

Quarter Back

A library employee from Portland State University admitted that she had stolen more than $200,000 over the years from the school's copy machines. According to the school's newspaper, the *Vanguard,* the woman begged for mercy, citing, in her defense, that she was just temporarily using the money anyway. The woman claimed that she had spent almost the entire amount on Oregon's government-sponsored video poker machines, and since she never won more than she put in, the state eventually got all its money back.

A young, attractive housewife from Melbourne, Australia, has been charged with animal cruelty in the shooting death of her neighbor's German shepherd. The woman argued that the dog provoked her by invading her **"personal space"** and that she acted in her own defense when she killed it with her husband's shotgun. What had the dog done? He sniffed up her miniskirt when she was not wearing any underwear.

Fire the First Volley

The New York Appellate Division of the Supreme Court unanimously revoked a lower court's award of $15 million to a Richmond Hill High School student who is paralyzed from the waist down. The New York City schoolboy was horsing around before volleyball practice and, when the coach left the auditorium, leapt over the volleyball net and landed on his head, breaking his neck. The student explained why he thought he was entitled to the enormous settlement by saying, "I accept part of the blame, but what about the responsibility of the teacher and the school?"

— — — — — — — — —

```
When he's sober, he's very much
   against drinking and driving.
```

—Attorney for the founder of Students Against Drinking and Driving at Calgary University, in response to his client's second drunken driving offense

Hey, Idiot!

Please Identify Yourself

As reported in the University of Arizona student newspaper, the *Arizona Daily Wildcat,* in their Police Beat column, a nineteen-year-old student filed a charge against a fellow student accusing him of stealing his fake Arizona driver's license. The complainant confessed that he had loaned the man the card, but after it was confiscated at a local club, the borrower refused to reimburse the complainant the $40 he'd paid for it. And remember, kids, I.D. are the first two letters in the word "idiot"!

A man in Hazard, Kentucky, divorced his wife because she **"beat him whenever he removed onions from his hamburger without first asking for permission."**

Ebony and Ivory

According to an article in the *Chicago Sun-Times,* a University of Pennsylvania student group, White Women Against Racism, excluded a black woman who expressed an interest in joining the group. A spokesperson for the group explained that whites have to meet among fellow whites in order to understand why they so often exclude blacks. "Racism is a white problem, and we have a responsibility as white women in particular to do what we can to eradicate racism." I guess these women don't think separating whites from colors only applies to doing laundry.

In Nice, France, a woman was injured when **she accidentally drove her car off a thirty-foot cliff.** The woman was in a hurry to go home to tell her family the good news—that she had recently been hired as a driving instructor.

One Toke over the Line

Judge Philip Mangones in Keene, New Hampshire, declared unconstitutional a dormitory search of two Keene State College students. The students agreed to allow authorities to search their room and when more than six ounces of marijuana was found the two students were arrested. The judge ruled in favor of the boys, stating that they were too stoned to know what they were doing when they consented to the search. Sounds like what happens when smoke gets in your eyes.

> Had I not been born with breasts, I would not have been prosecuted. It's not for attention. It's for civil rights.
>
> —*A Texas woman who was convicted of disorderly conduct after she bared her breasts at Sylvan Beach in La Porte*

Hey, Idiot!

Press to Dispense Justice

A man in Eureka, California, was caught on surveillance cameras stealing coins from a soda vending machine. Apparently thirsty after stealing all the cold, hard cash, the man put some of the change back into the machine to get a drink. The soda machine malfunctioned and didn't dispense his drink. Outraged at the machine and how it had "eaten his money" the thief, still caught on tape, mind you, wrote a note on the machine with his name and phone number and the amount of money the machine owed him. I wonder if during his arraignment he paid his bond entirely in quarters.

The excuse offered up by a thirty-five-year-old man accused of stabbing his wife to death—the strange sediment from a **bottle of ice tea he drank caused him to attack her with a knife.**

Pool Rules

A woman in Hamilton, Ontario, who was breast-feeding her daughter in a swimming pool at a local public recreation center was ordered out of the pool by the lifeguard on duty. "I was sitting in the pool with my daughter in front of me, and I pulled down my bathing suit strap and took out my breast and put her on it," said the twenty-five-year-old mother. The lifeguard suggested the woman remove herself and the feeding child from the pool and go into a changing room. Authorities for the pool said the woman was breaking the recreation department's rule, not against indecent exposure, but for having "food or drink" in the pool. Sounds to me like the baby was just practicing her breaststroke.

When a prominent Canadian geneticist told residents of a remote village in Newfoundland that they possessed a genetic flaw that increased their chances of heart disease— they were happy. **"This is great!"** several residents said. "This means we're doomed, so we . . . don't need to quit smoking or [stop eating fatty foods]."

Gentleman Bandit

A man accused of robbing $3,000 from a New Jersey bank filed a $1.2 million defamation lawsuit against the bank teller whom he robbed. The alleged bank robber filed his suit from prison, where he was awaiting trial. The suit claims that the teller defamed and slandered him by telling police he had threatened to shoot her if she didn't hand over the money. The accused robber said he was deeply hurt by her slanderous words because he never threatened to shoot her and simply handed her a very polite note that read, "I want the money now." What, no "please"?

A grand jury didn't believe the sequence of events that led to the death of a Soldotna, Alaska, man. The accused murderer said he awoke to find his cousin flailing on the floor in mortal agony from a self-inflicted gunshot. And instead of calling 911, **he decided the humane thing to do was to finish him off.** He was indicted on charges of first-degree murder.

Hey, Idiot!

As God Is My Witness

We've all, at one point or another, wanted to blame other people for our problems. Well, a Pennsylvania man took that one step further when he filed a lawsuit claiming someone else was responsible for his problems—God. The man claimed that God the Almighty failed to bring him justice in a thirty-year-old legal battle with his former employer. His claim was that "Defendant God is the sovereign ruler of the universe and took no corrective action against extremely serious wrongs, which ruined [my] life. . . ." He probably thought he would hedge his bets by including a few other codicils just in case he was victorious. In addition to accepting that he was responsible for the man's failures in life, God was also required to return the man's youth and bestow upon him guitar-playing skills equal to those of Eric Clapton, B.B. King, and other guitar greats. And while God was doing that he could also resurrect the man's mother and pet pigeon. For some reason, a judge threw the case out before it even got a hearing. My guess is that the judge realized that God wasn't a resident of Pennsylvania or even a citizen of the United States, and therefore couldn't be called into court. Or am I just talking crazy?

A passenger who allegedly attacked and injured a Continental Airlines ticket agent is suing the airlines for the company's **"poor training"** of its employees.

Boxers or Briefs?

An eighteen-year-old motorist was seen driving erratically and was pulled over by police. The man bolted from his car, and police pursued him on foot, caught him, and placed him in the back of their patrol car to take him downtown for a Breathalyzer test. Once he was alone in the backseat, the young man knew he had to do something, so he ripped the crotch out of his underwear and stuffed it into his mouth. He did so believing that the cotton would absorb all the alcohol, but surprisingly—it didn't. He tested positive for alcohol and was arrested. Ultimately he was acquitted of drunk driving charges, but his testimony caused so much laughter in the courtroom that many members of the court had to be escorted out in tears. I'm glad the accused man didn't offer anything on which to wipe their eyes.

— — — — — — — — —

```
I can't help it, Officer. Someone has
   hypnotized me to park illegally.
```

—*Excuse offered up by the driver of an illegally parked car*

Can't Deal with It

A man playing blackjack became so enraged when he lost forty-six straight hands to the same blackjack dealer that he shot her to death. His explanation of the events went like this: "I was betting fairly heavy . . . no matter what I did she found a way to beat me. I'd get a nineteen and she'd get a twenty. I'd get a twenty, she'd get a twenty-one. It was totally unreal. . . . Finally I just went crazy and blew that smile right off her face. . . . The next thing I knew, the police were hauling me to jail. I guess it just wasn't my lucky day." Maybe the judge, if he has any sense of humor, will sentence the man to twenty-one years to life.

A judge had a hard time believing the excuse offered up by a man accused of allowing his automobile to lunge forward, nearly hitting a police officer, during a traffic stop. The man claimed that he wasn't driving the car at the time and blamed his two dogs. **The man said one dog pressed the gas pedal while the other dog put the car into gear.**

A Titillating Excuse

An elementary school teacher from Palm Harbor, Florida, was arrested on suspicion of driving under the influence and was dismissed from her job. The woman successfully beat the conviction and was reinstated by the school board as a result. The woman argued, apparently convincingly, that the reason she appeared disoriented during the stop wasn't because she was drunk, but because a silicone breast implant ruptured and poisoned her nervous system. Now if Pamela Anderson is ever pulled over she'll know she has a full set of excuses.

I just spent a lot of money getting my brakes repaired, and I didn't want to wear them down.

—*Excuse given for speeding to Andersonville, Illinois, police officer*

She Didn't Leave Home Without It

A Marin County, California, woman is fighting her credit card companies in their attempt to recover more than $70,000 in charges. The woman became addicted to gambling over the Internet and ran up credit card charges on both her Visa and MasterCard but won't even pay the minimum due. Not only has she refused to pay the credit card companies but she has now filed a countersuit against them claiming that because gambling is illegal in California, her credit card companies shouldn't have allowed the charges to go through in the first place. Do you think she'll be successful? Don't bet on it.

Crown Point, Indiana, police have finally reopened the case of a man who died from thirty-two hammer blows to his head. **Police ruled the cause of death as a suicide.** The county coroner's opinion is that a person could not remain conscious long enough to hit himself in the head thirty-two times.

Ask and Ye Shall Receive

"**W**hen I read it, I was taken aback," said the lawyer representing the Federal National Mortgage Association. The attorney was talking about a response from two customers refusing to pay their $54,000 mortgage even though they were facing foreclosure. The married couple claimed they didn't have to pay the money, and they got that from the highest source possible—God. "It was our desire to be free from this mortgage debt," the couple told a court handling their foreclosure. "Therefore, we asked God our Heavenly Father in the name of Jesus Christ. He heard us, and he freed us from this mortgage bondage." I know God had Moses tell the Egyptians, "Let my people go," but I don't remember him saying, "Let my people go debt-free."

We aren't criminals. If we had gotten away with it, it would never have happened again.

—*A twenty-one-year-old man accused, along with his partner, of beating a woman to death and then running over her with a car*

More Than the Market Can Bare

A graduate student from Indianapolis filed a complaint against the Ameritrade discount brokerage claiming that the company should absolve him of his $40,000 debt. The student began eagerly trading stock on-line, borrowing money to buy stocks "on margin" without reading Ameritrade's special margin-trading instructions. When the stock market plunged the student lost his entire medical-school nest egg of $40,000. He said he "never dreamt I had any possibility of losing all my money." The student doesn't think it's fair and now would like the stock-trading giant to give him a break and give him the money back. That reasoning is pure bullish (wait, did I spell that right?).

He stares at me and "my girl"
while we're on the couch.

—*Excuse given at a humane shelter by a man turning in a dog*

The Anytime Teller

A thirty-four-year-old man was arrested and charged with holding up the Palmetto Bank in Spartanburg, South Carolina. During his trial the man admitted that he had robbed the bank but claimed he did so because he had been erroneously charged $600 in overdraft fees because of a mix-up with his student loan. His story didn't go over with the judges, however, because the man's bank is the First Federal Bank, not the Palmetto Bank. The man tried to talk his way around that issue by claiming that he really wanted to rob the First Federal Bank but that the Palmetto Bank was the only bank open on the Saturday when he got the idea to get his money back. Looks like this fellow is going to get "a substantial penalty for early withdrawal."

Arguing his case via a letter in the school newspaper, a University of New Hampshire business major blamed his recent drunken driving arrest on a police crackdown on underage drinking. The underage student complained that since he now has to drive to another city to drink, **"I can expect to be doing a lot more drunk driving."**

Hey, Idiot!

Leave a Message and I'll Get Back to You

A man convicted in Hartford, Connecticut, of defrauding investors of $4.8 million sent a letter to U.S. marshals telling them that he wouldn't be going to jail as they had planned. The man's letter stated that he felt he had made a strong case for his innocence during trial and that instead of going to prison as ordered he would be vacationing with some relatives near Syracuse, New York. He mentioned that if he didn't hear back from the marshals, he would consider the case closed. He did hear from the marshals when they knocked on the door to rearrest him. During his trial, the man again told authorities that he should be released for two reasons: one, he considered himself a "sovereign" and not subject to U.S. laws; and two, in the indictment, prosecutors had spelled his name in all capitals. He won't have to worry about someone spelling his name in all caps anymore—from now on his name is going to be spelled in all numbers.

"Pseudologia Fantastica": a medical condition offered up by doctors in defense of a Los Angeles **judge accused of padding his résumé with lies.**

Governmental
Idiots

Hey, Idiot!

Snail Mail

We've all heard the expression "The check's in the mail," but for 2,600 state employees whose weekly paychecks got lost in the mail, the joke was on them—they were all postal employees. In Norfolk, Virginia, postal employees awaited their last paycheck of the year, eagerly anticipating getting their check deposited before the banks closed for the holidays. But (ah, delicious irony) the post office lost its own mail. The checks did arrive—two days late and too late for the employees to get to the bank. "We're sure that irony will not be lost on folks," said Bruce Threatte, finance director at the Norfolk post office. Where were the checks for those few extra days? No one seems to know. The frightening thing is that at one time, there were 2,600 disgruntled postal employees in one place.

After construction of the seventeen-ton Compton Gamma-Ray Observatory **satellite went $40 million over budget,** NASA sent a $5 million bonus check to the contractor.

To Thy Own Self Be Sued

After defeat in his congressional race, Arkansas Secretary of State Bill McCuen challenged the results of the election with a lawsuit, claiming irregularities in the voting process. The twist is, since vote administration in Arkansas is under the control of the secretary of state's office, McCuen was forced to file the lawsuit against—himself.

The only way we'll ever get a volunteer army is to draft them.

—*F. Edward Hébert, former chairman of the House Committee on Armed Services*

Hey, Idiot!

Easier Said Than Done

The following excerpt is from the *U.S. Government Peace Corps Manual* for volunteers working in the Amazon jungle, detailing what to do if an anaconda attacks you:

> Related to the boa constrictor, the anaconda is the largest snake species in the world. It grows to thirty-five feet in length and weighs three hundred to four hundred pounds.
>
> 1. If you are attacked by an anaconda, do not run. The snake is faster than you are.
>
> 2. Lie flat on the ground. Put your arms tight against your sides, your legs tight against one another.
>
> 3. Tuck your chin in.
>
> 4. The snake will begin to nudge and climb over your body.
>
> 5. Do not panic.

6. After the snake has examined you, it will begin to swallow you from the feet end—always from the feet end. Permit the snake to swallow your feet and ankles. Do not panic!

7. The snake will now begin to suck your legs into its body. You must lie perfectly still. This will take a long time.

8. When the snake has reached your knees, slowly and with as little movement as possible, reach down, take your knife and very gently slide it into the side of the snake's mouth between the edge of its mouth and your leg, then suddenly rip upward, severing the snake's head.

9. Be sure you have your knife.

10. Be sure your knife is sharp.

Hey, Idiot!

Scrooged Again

A lot of people claim state government employees are lazy, and usually those people are right. But in one case, Millie Wood was punished for not being lazy enough. Wood, seventy-two, was suspended for one day without pay after decorating a Christmas tree. You see, for the past twelve years, Wood had put up a Christmas tree in the lobby of the town clerk's office in Wallingford, Connecticut. Tax Collector Norman Rosow told Wood not to put up and decorate the tree that year, but Wood did it anyway, on her own time, and was suspended because of it. Town officials claim the issue isn't the tree; it's a matter of ignoring a supervisor's instructions. In a classic case of bureaucratic idiocy, they stated their position that it might cause the town to pay overtime and also raise liability questions. What did the townspeople think about the council's actions? They lined up to donate money to a candy basket at the clerk's office to help Millie Wood make up her lost day's pay. Now that's what Christmas is all about.

Into the Air, Junior Birdsmen

We've all seen the awesome weapons and equipment developed by the United States Government—smart bombs, Humvees, etc.—but have you ever heard of the "birdstrike simulator"? No. In order to determine how well the canopies of jet aircraft will stand up after mid-air collision with a bird (something that happens very frequently), the Air Force developed the "birdstrike simulator," also known as the chicken gun. Using a converted twenty-foot cannon, four-pound chickens (yes, they're dead) are loaded up and fired directly into a parked plane's windshield; at speeds of seven hundred miles an hour the frequent fryers simulate the impact of a real bird caught in flight. The damage is investigated and modifications are made to enhance a windshield's ability to absorb the impact. All went well until one private, and this is true, loaded the gun with frozen chickens.

As artist Jack Dowd prepared to exhibit his life-sized bronze sculpture *Man & His Dog* in Tompkins Square Park in New York City, city officials reminded him of New York's strict leash laws. They wanted to make sure the "dog" would be tethered to its owner with a bronze leash.

Hey, Idiot!

The Bear Necessities

Montana rancher John Shuler was having trouble with grizzly bears mauling and killing his sheep. One night he awoke to the sounds of terrified sheep, and he knew the bears were back. He grabbed his rifle and went outside. He saw three grizzlies attacking his sheep—then he turned to see a fourth bear coming after him. He quickly shouldered his rifle and fired, killing the bear. The Interior Department heard about the incident and sued Shuler under the Endangered Species Act. Shuler was dragged before one of the agency's administrative law judges, who found him at fault because "he purposefully placed himself in the zone of imminent danger." For the act of protecting his sheep and saving his own life, John Shuler was fined $4,000. My question is: Why does the Interior Department only deal with things on the outside?

Their Bark Is Worse Than Their Bite

Birch trees in national forests in Minnesota were being stripped of their bark by lazy campers looking for easy firewood to burn. The U.S. Forest Service was called in and immediately jumped into action. Did the rangers lie in wait and arrest campers stripping the trees? Nope. They sent workers into the woods armed with buckets of whitewash to paint the bark white like birches. After the paint was dry, a second coat was applied consisting of dark pigments used to imitate bark and—completing the faux flora—realistic knotholes. Hmmm, knotholes—sounds like a pretty good description of whoever came up with this idea.

The voters have spoken—the bastards.

—*Morris Udall, acknowledging his loss in the 1976 presidential primary election*

Hey, Idiot!

The Blind Leading the Blind

The Texas Commission for the Blind, whose sole responsibility is to supply support for the visually impaired in the workplace, was charged by the U.S. Department of Justice with discrimination. The Commission for the Blind was found guilty of issuing printed employee manuals but not making available Braille or large-type versions for its sight-impaired workers. They were forced to pay $55,000 to settle the claims. So the commission was both out of sight and out of mind.

A small metal-forming shop in Chicago was cited by the Equal Employment Opportunity Commission for hiring too many Hispanic and Polish-American workers and no blacks. The EEOC forced the company to run an advertisement inviting blacks to file claims for compensation on the basis of discrimination. **One hundred and twenty-seven were awarded payouts**—even if they had never applied for a job at that company.

Hey, Idiot!

The Green House Effect

The City Council of Joliet, Illinois, passed an ordinance requiring builders to make houses less similar by forcing them to use a variety of colors and aesthetic features. One of the council members who supported the ordinance, Councilor Joseph Shetina, stated that the requirement was necessary because, "You go home drunk, and you'd never know which house was yours."

— — — — — — — — —

I do believe we spend a lot of time doing very little, and that may be an understatement.

—Robert Dole (R-Kansas) on Congress

Hey, Idiot!

A Real Bunch of Nuts

The Agriculture Department's Food and Safety Inspection Service defines "mixed nuts" as "the food consisting of a mixture of four or more of the optional shelled tree nut ingredients, with or without one or more of the optional shelled peanut ingredients, of the kinds prescribed by paragraph (b) of this section. . . . When two ounces or less of the food is packed in transparent containers, three or more of the optional tree nut ingredients shall be present. . . . Each such kind of nut ingredient when used shall be present in a quantity not less than 2 percent and not more than 80 percent by weight of the finished food." Nuts can include almonds, black walnuts, Brazil nuts, cashews, English walnuts, filberts, pecans, other suitable tree nuts, and peanut varieties such as Spanish, Valencia, Virginia, "or any combination of two or more such varieties." Now, that was simple enough, wasn't it?

Mind Your Own Dam Business

The Michigan Department of Environmental Quality, acting on the complaint of a neighbor, sent a letter to a Montcalm County resident informing him that he lacked the proper permits on his "construction and maintenance of two wood debris dams across the outlet stream of Spring Pond." They also warned him against any further "unauthorized activity" in connection with the above-mentioned structure. The landowner shot back a response to the department denying their authority to control the building of the structures. The department immediately investigated and soon realized that the dams had been built by beavers.

Traditionally, most of Australia's imports come from overseas.

—*Former Australian cabinet minister Keppel Enderbery*

Hey, Idiot!

Power-balling the State

In these days of homeland security, it's nice to know that our government is at the ready. But ready or not, the state of Oregon paid $124,700 to a Virginia firm for a disaster preparedness plan that would keep the state's lottery system active even in the event of a major earthquake. A lottery spokesman defended the expenditure by stating the importance of keeping the games up and running even during a natural disaster because it generates $1 million a day in revenues for the state. Wow, a lottery lobbyist defending the lottery—what are the odds?

The following are excerpts from a farm-safety pamphlet issued by the Occupational Safety and Health Administration: "Hazards are one of the main causes of accidents. A hazard is anything that is dangerous." Later the publication warned, **"Be careful that you do not fall into the manure pits."**

Hey, Idiot!

Suffering from Heat Stroke

Nebraska state officials were surprised to receive a letter from the Environmental Protection Agency indicating that the state might have to seek action against a polluter for raising water temperatures. The letter went on to explain that the polluter's actions were responsible for reducing the water quality along much of the length of the Platte River. Was it some major conglomerate or an eco-terrorist polluting the water? No, actually, as far as the puzzled politicians could figure out, the perpetrator was—the sun. Officials interpreted the EPA's letter as meaning they might have to take action against the sun in the form of piping in colder water or even installing a shield or canopies to shade the waterway.

The General Accounting Office noted that while frozen cheese **pizzas were inspected by the Food and Drug Administration,** those with meat toppings were inspected by the Department of Agriculture.

Hey, Idiot!

Jamaica Mistake?

The following excerpts are from *Rezedents Rights & Rispansabilities,* a pamphlet using dialect translation distributed to Caribbean tenants by the Department of Housing and Urban Development.

> Yuh as a rezedent, ave di rights ahn di rispansabilities to elp mek yuh HUD-assisted owzing ah behta owme fi yuh ahn yuh fambily. Dis brochure briefly liss some ahf yuh muos impowtant rights ahn rispansabilities fi elp yuh get di muos owt ah yuh owme.
>
> Yuh Rights:
>
> • Di right fi get reasonable notice, in writing fi ehni non-imergency inspeckshan aur ehni ahdah entry inna yuh apawtment.
>
> • Di right fi puoss materials in cammon areas fi infawm ahdah rezedents bout dem rights ahn also about apportunities ahf ow dem caan invalve demself in deir projeks.
>
> • Di rights fi recognition by prahpaty ownas ahn manigahs as smady dat ave a seh in rezedenshal community affairs.

HUD withdrew the pamphlet after receiving numerous complaints. No shehtmon.

The Land of the Free

The Agency for International Development spent $12 million educating Tunisian students in the United States so they would return to their homeland and enrich their fellow countrymen with their newfound knowledge. An impressive seventy students earned doctorate degrees at the expense of the United States government, but instead of going back home they all decided to stay in the United States instead. And people say there's no such thing as a free lunch.

"The way we travel is damaging our towns, harming our countryside, and changing the climate of the planet," said Labor MP Alan Meale, an environmental official with the British government. His speech at a conference on automobile pollution in Peterborough, England, ran out of gas when the politician was seen riding the short two-mile distance from the railroad station to the meeting in a Lincoln stretch limousine.

Hey, Idiot!

Spell Check, Anyone?

The following are direct excerpts from a memo that accompanied the Goals 2000 education program to Congress:

This has been espeically true in education over the past decades.

The Education America Act sets into law the six National Education Goals and establishe a bipartisan National Eduation Goals Panel to report on progress towards acheiveing the goals.

It is time to rekindle the dream that good shools offer.

Oh, now I know why Johnny can't read.

Vermont state representative Robert Kinsey introduced a **bill to require CPR training as a condition for a marriage license.**

Earth, Wind, and Fire

We all remember the disastrous voting fiasco that took place during the 2000 presidential election; who could forget chads, hanging chads, dimpled chads, and the rest of the embarrassing voting disasters. But there was a clear winner between the candidates for the board of the Soil and Water Conservation District in Volusia County, Florida, even though their names didn't appear on the ballot because of late filings. Underneath the board's name, the ballot instructed the voter to "choose one" and "write in." Of the thousands of votes cast for the two apparent candidates, "Soil" or "Water," the winner, by a large margin was—Water. There's no word on whether Soil will ask for a recount. And remember, those were the people's numbers, those weren't Water's numbers.

An AIDS-awareness drive distributed thousands of government-issued safe sex packs to South Africans, which included free condoms and information about AIDS. The packs were soon discarded when it was discovered that **the free condoms had been attached to the pamphlets with staples.**

Hey, Idiot!

Say What?

Surgeon Fay Boozman, current Arkansas State Health director for the U.S. Senate, said during his failed campaign for a proposed abortion bill that a "rape exception" was not necessary because fear triggers a natural contraceptive chemical in the woman that prevents conception. He did not produce research but said his statement was based on general knowledge in the medical community. Boozman lost the election to Blanche Lincoln, a woman, after unprecedented female voter turnout.

— — — — — — — — — —

```
We cannot move forward by running
constantly to the right or to the left.
Sometimes we need less government,
    and sometimes we need more.
```

—Senator Edward Kennedy

Hey, Idiot!

Do What I Say Not as I Do

City officials in Des Moines, Iowa, are unhappy with all the paper notices, flyers, and garage sale signs that hang from utility poles for weeks. "It looks really tacky," Councilman Michael McPherson said. So they busily drafted legislation that would bar signs from being posted on utility poles. And to make sure everyone gets the news, they're posting signs that say it's illegal to post signs on utility poles.

— — — — — — — — —

```
     Now, we talked to Joan Hanover.
   She and her husband, George, were
     visiting with us. They are near
  retirement--retiring--in the process
    of retiring, meaning they're very
  smart, active, capable people who are
     retirement age and are retiring.
```

—George W. Bush, Alexandria, Virginia, February 12, 2003

Hey, Idiot!

No Publicity Is Bad Publicity...
Well...

Dorothy Jennings, a candidate for mayor in Baltimore, Maryland, appeared on a local news show to discuss her campaign. When she started talking about one of her campaign themes, crime, something sounded familiar to an off-duty police officer watching the show. He recognized Jennings not as a mayoral candidate but as Dorothy Joyner, a woman he knew was wanted for burglary. He alerted the local precinct, which sent in several police officers, who arrested Jennings/Joyner and led her out of the studio in handcuffs. Film at eleven.

A Florida strip club owner petitioned the state because **he was having difficulty finding local women willing to perform as exotic dancers.** He asked the state to provide work visas for foreign women so he could keep his customers happy. But in order to stay within the bounds of immigration law, the state first had to place ads for exotic dancers in various newspapers to make sure no Americans were available to fill the positions.

Medical
Idiots

An Ear-itating Incident

A young girl in Kenya somehow managed to get a bean lodged in her ear, and she couldn't get it out. Her family took her to their local doctor, who, in a matter of minutes, had the lodged legume removed. The grateful family thanked the doctor and he, in turn, handed the family the bill for his services—350 shillings (equivalent to $5.75). When the embarrassed family explained they only had 270 shillings, the doctor grabbed the girl and stuck the bean back into her ear. The Kenya Medical Association is investigating the incident. Now, I've heard of cauliflower ears before but . . .

The Consumer Product Safety Commission's report on sports injuries concluded that 1,455 people were sent to emergency rooms in 1992 with **injuries suffered from playing Ping-Pong.**

Salad on the Half Shell

We've all heard jokes about the poor quality of hospital food, but one lady recuperating in Iowa Lutheran Hospital in Des Moines didn't see the humor in finding a dead bird in her spinach. She knew the bird was dead because the first bite she took out of her meal included the bird's head. "The immediate effect was nausea, but she still has a hard time even talking about it two years later," said the woman's attorney. "Spinach used to be one of her favorite foods." To make matters worse, her attorney claimed, the hospital continued to serve her spinach after the bird incident. Even Popeye wouldn't be strong enough to stomach that.

Nurse Bobbie Heaney filed a lawsuit claiming that she and Dr. William McIntosh got into an argument following a delivery, and **he squirted her in the face with blood** from an umbilical cord.

Laboring Under a Misapprehension

A pregnant woman from Ontario, Canada, sued her doctors and McMaster Hospital for $2.4 million. Did they remove the wrong leg, or was it another bird in the spinach salad? No, the woman sued because she had pain while giving birth. She claimed her doctors promised that her birth would be "so pain-free, she could knit or read a book during the procedure." But the pain was so traumatizing, the woman testified, she had "intrusive thoughts"—believing, for example, the hospital had secretly called her dentist and asked him to make sure "I have as much pain as possible during dental treatment." The woman, whose husband happens to be a physician at McMaster (wink, wink), said she filed the suit not for the money but "to make sure this doesn't happen to anyone else." I'll tell you one thing; she sure is lucky she didn't have her baby in Kenya!

Patient failed to fulfill
his wellness potential.

—*Final notation on the chart of a patient who passed away*

Let's Take a Look at Your Chart

The following are actual diagnostic notations given by doctors.

- The patient is married but sexually active.

- She does indeed have fear of frying and mental problems which she attributes to deep fat fryers.

- The patient's father died at age sixty-five, but he has not been seen for some time.

- The patient has crap in his cast with walking. [Instead of "cramps in his calves."]

- With standing with eyes closed, he missed his right finger to his nose and has to search for it on the left side.

- The patient is a fifty-three-year-old police officer who was found unconscious by his bicycle.

- Her father died from a heart attack at age twelve.

A Las Vegas hospital suspended several workers for
betting on when patients would die.

Just Put One Foot
in Front of the Other...

Imagine the horror of having one of your legs surgically amputated, then imagine the horror of waking up after surgery
and discovering the doctor removed your healthy leg instead.
That's just what happened to Willie King at the University
Community Hospital in Tampa, Florida. The surgery was performed by Dr. Rolando Sanchez—well, the first surgery, that is.
King later had to have his other leg amputated at a different
hospital. He sued both the hospital and Dr. Sanchez and was
awarded $1,150,000. After this surgical screwup, the hospital
started a new policy of writing the word "no" on patients' limbs
that are not supposed to be amputated. Too bad they didn't
write the word "no" on patients' toes. Five months after Dr.
Sanchez took off the wrong leg, he removed the toe of a woman
without consent. The woman entered the Town and Country
Hospital to have dead tissue removed from her right foot
(a procedure known as debridement). An emergency order
from the state Agency for Health Care Administration said
that Dr. Sanchez "presents an immediate and serious danger to
the health, safety and welfare of the public." The order went
on to explain the situation: "In preparation for the procedure,
Dr. Sanchez requested a bone cutter from a surgical nurse, as
he 'might have to take off a toe.' The nurse asked Dr. Sanchez
if the consent form should include consent for amputation of
the toe and Dr. Sanchez stated 'no.'" After Sanchez amputated

Hey, Idiot!

the patient's toe he later denied his actions "stating that it had fallen off." Dr. Sanchez's medical license was suspended, but don't worry about him not making any money. Why? Because he filed a lawsuit against the city over a jogging accident in which he broke his arm after falling into a hole cut away for a sprinkler system. I suggest the good doctor write the word "no" on the arm he doesn't want put into a cast.

-- -- -- -- -- -- -- -- -- --

```
   Every person now living in the
 United States has one chance out of
   fourteen of dying of tuberculosis
 and one chance in fifty of becoming
      affected with this disease.
```

—*Managing director of the National Tuberculosis Association, Dr. Linsly R. Williams, as quoted in the* Congressional Record

No Thanks, I'm Stuffed

Goeran Rudolfsson of Stockholm, Sweden, had been bothered by nasal congestion since having an operation on a brain tumor a few months before. He sniffed, snorted, and took cold medicine, but nothing seemed to help. Grabbing his handkerchief one day, he blew his nose extremely hard, hoping to clear his nasal passages. When he took the handkerchief away he felt something hanging out of his nose. Using his forefinger and thumb he grasped the object and tugged—it turned out to be a thirty-one-inch-long cloth. The cloth had been placed in his head during the operation to absorb fluids and had accidentally been left there. Rudolfsson removed the cloth himself by slowly pulled the rag until it was fully out of his nose. Rudolfsson can breathe a little easier now, but I bet the hospital's lawyers are holding their breath.

The maternity ward at Rockyview Hospital in Calgary, Alberta, stopped loaning black ink pens (required to fill out their birthing paperwork) and **charged women twenty-five cents each** to buy them.

If You Need Anything Just Pull My Finger

A nurse in Ontario, Canada, has been found guilty of misconduct for purposely passing gas in front of a patient's wife. After the first breaking of wind, the nurse sneered and asked the woman if she "wanted more," before letting another one rip. This isn't the first time the nurse has been reprimanded, and she has a history of "demeaning and unprofessional" behavior. Another incident included the following comment made to a bedridden patient who asked the registered nurse for assistance in getting out of bed: "I don't know why she wants to get up. All she does all day is sit on her ass and spit all over her clothes." Nurse Ratched, you're wanted on floor three. Nurse Ratched to floor three, please.

In December 1995 a **surgeon removed an inch-long tree sprig** from the right lung of a sixteen-year-old Stockton, California, girl, who'd apparently inhaled it in 1980 from the family Christmas tree. The sprig, which miraculously was still green, was apparently the source of the girl's notorious problems with halitosis.

Hey, Idiot!

Refusing to Pass Gas

An anesthesiologist from Wilkes-Barre, Pennsylvania, was arrested and sentenced to ten to twenty-three months in prison. The doctor pleaded guilty to diluting the anesthesia of patients in order to feed his own drug habit. He was suspected after a number of patients complained of excruciating pain during their operations. Let's see, a patient complaining of excruciating pain when they're supposed to be under anesthesia—yeah, that would have clued me in.

— — — — — — — — — —

```
I've done everything from horses down
  to chickens, hogs, cats, and goats.
   I've treated them all, including
        members of my family.
```

—Acupuncturist H. Grady Young

Unsportsmanlike Conduct

Occasionally when someone is taken to a trauma center, the doctor is delayed in coming to the patient's aid because of another crisis. Sometimes the crisis is real and immediate, and other times it's just bull—or should I say Bulls? A seventy-six-year-old woman was taken to a hospital in Chicago suffering from cardiac arrest, but the specialist on call refused to come to the hospital because the Chicago Bulls were playing the Utah Jazz in the NBA Playoffs. Another specialist on call had a family matter to attend to. The patient was transported to another hospital, and unfortunately she died en route. The woman's family is suing the hospital, and I have a feeling the ball will be in their court in court.

While visiting the family doctor in Stuart, Florida, a fifty-eight-year-old man dislodged a cherry pit from his nose during a routine examination. He explained to his doctor that **he used to stuff cherry pits up his nose to impress his friends,** but the last time he did that was when he was eight years old. His doctor claimed that this might be the longest period that an object ever remained in someone's nose.

Hey, Idiot!

Strange Bedside Manners

A doctor had been sued by a nurse, found guilty, and ordered to pay $5,000 by a jury in New Orleans. The nurse claimed the doctor shot her in the buttocks with a surgical staple gun as a "joke." She testified that while she was bending over to gather sponges, the doctor shot her in the butt with the gun he had only moments before used to close a surgical wound.

Ah, the Life of the Actor

The University of Toronto's medical school employs actors and other people to be "practice patients" for its students. The stand-in sickies get paid between $12 and $35 an hour, depending on their experience and their phony conditions. For example, Bob LeRoy commands the top of the pay scale owing to the fact that he is a rectal-exam patient. The forty-five-year-old LeRoy said with a grimace, "I always hope the student with the biggest finger goes first."

Hey, Idiot!

Open for Lunch

A neurosurgeon had his practice suspended because of nine separate incidents, including one where he left in the middle of aneurysm surgery. The brain surgeon (and I use the word only in its technical sense) left the patient alone with his brain exposed so he could take a lunch break. The wise and wonderful people on the state medical board in Wilmington, North Carolina, ruled that the doctor might practice again provided he continues undergoing psychiatric and medical evaluations. Looks like there are quite a few people in this world in need of a little brain surgery.

No Children Allowed

—A sign in a hospital maternity ward

Let's Take a Look at Your Chart, Too

Here are more actual doctors' notes.

- A sensation of an awareness of a feeling of a decreased sensation.

- Shortly after the surgery, he turned into an emergency room.

- She is rather petite with a height measured today of 6'4" and weight of 100 pounds.

- So far as I could tell, she has not had any significant illnesses in her past life.

- At this time he was felling trees and in the process of a tree falling on another tree he was hit by a tree and thrown face first against another tree.

- His legs do not seem to keep him from walking.

Obaid Mubarak bin Suwaidan Bal-Jaflah of Dubai, United Arab Emirates, **died a few days after his first and only visit to a doctor**—he was 135 years old.

A Real Hospital Chain

Reuters News Service reported that not only seven women but also eight newborn babies were being held in Kinshasa, Zaire, at the King Baudoin Hospital. Some of the hostages had been held for as long as three months because they were unable to pay their maternity bills. A spokesperson for the hospital said, "We are obliged to use unusual means to force the patients to find the money." And you thought HMOs were tough to deal with.

The chief surgeon at a Shriners Burn Institute was investigated because it was heard that **he drew "happy faces" on the penises of two patients.** He was cleared of any charges because one of the patients testified that the surgeon's actions added a little humor to the otherwise stressful situation of surgery. "I'll let him draw another anytime," the patient said.

Registered Nurse

Authorities in Hershey, Pennsylvania, have accused a former nurse of stealing from a patient. Was the woman rifling through purses or dipping into unconscious men's wallets looking for cash? Nope, she allegedly stole a Beanie Baby toy from a twelve-year-old girl who was recovering from open-heart surgery. The fifty-year-old nurse struggled with officers when they tried to confiscate "Halo, the angel bear," which the nurse had stolen from the girl's bedside. She was arrested for theft, resisting arrest, and disorderly conduct. Maybe Tyco will come out with "Parolee, the ex-convict bear" in honor of the nurse.

In an effort to downsize services at its emergency room, Kidderminster Hospital in Worcestershire, England, sent out a pamphlet to 100,000 local families. Among other things, **the pamphlet advises people that if they fall into a coma, they should request that the ambulance take them to other hospitals.**

Hey, Idiot!

Trip Down Memory Lane

A forty-four-year-old woman claims to have suffered memory loss as a result of severe head-banging on an amusement ride at Six Flags Elitch Gardens in Denver, Colorado. "I could have a conversation with someone and turn around and have no memory of it," the woman said. "I would lose time. I'd be standing at the stove with a spice in my hand and couldn't remember if I'd used it or not." She is suing the amusement park, claiming the ride is defective and resulted in her loss of memory. The roller coaster's name: Mind Eraser. Sounds like truth in advertising if you ask me.

A doctor at Mount Sinai Hospital in New York asked the shocked parents of a recently delivered baby if they had a desire to eat the placenta. **"I've had a few couples who wanted to do that,"** the doctor argued.

Hey, Idiot!

Open Wide and Say Ahhhhhhhhhhhhh!!!!!!

The term "painless dentistry" is about as realistic as "jumbo shrimp"—it's either one or the other. Just ask this Memphis, Tennessee, woman. The poor woman suffered from a gum disease and was told by her dentist that all of her teeth would have to be removed. She assumed the teeth would be extracted over a series of visits—her dentist had a different idea. He had yanked out nearly sixteen teeth and was going for all thirty-two when the woman finally fainted and had to be hospitalized for six days. She is suing the doctor for battery. I have a feeling that even though the woman doesn't have any teeth, her lawyer is going to take a bite out of this dentist's liability insurance.

An Oklahoma City jury awarded Mark Macsenti $1.3 million from his dentist Jon D. Becker. Macsenti suffered brain damage after Becker fell asleep during an appointment and left Mascenti hooked up to the nitrous oxide tank for nearly ten hours. Which just goes to show that **nitrous oxide is no laughing matter.**

Put a Sock in It

"**O**ften when people have a craving, it is because they are lacking something in their diet," said an associate professor of nutrition at the University of Buffalo. So it makes one wonder what could be missing in the diet of a particular twenty-two-year-old woman who suffers from a rare medical condition that makes her eat socks. The woman claims she consumes about half a sock each evening and that during her youth she routinely ate clothing. The medical condition is called pica, and is a disease where the sufferer craves nonfood items. So it's not just the clothes dryer that eats socks anymore.

"A Man Who Pricked His Finger and Smelled Putrid for Five Years."

—*Title of a medical journal paper by a British doctor*

Hey, Idiot!

The Nut Cracker Suite

A Detroit, Michigan, man is suing his chiropractor for pain and suffering, disfigurement, and consequential damages (i.e., the lack of sexual performance and/or enjoyment). The man was having a spinal adjustment for pain in his lower back. When the chiropractor adjusted the table, the man's genitals got caught in the fold of the table and were crushed. His lawyer expects to settle the lawsuit in the high "six figures." So he traded one digit for six.

A former patient sued the Davenport Medical Center in Davenport, Iowa, for **leaving a fourteen-by-fourteen-inch sponge in his abdomen** during gall bladder surgery. Authorities at the hospital believe and maintain that he swallowed it.

Chestnuts Roasting on an Open Fire

Things really heated up during a procedure to have a mole removed from the back of a Danish man. The man's genitals had been scrubbed with surgical spirits, and when the doctor began removing the mole with an electric knife, the patient inadvertently passed gas. A spark from the knife ignited the methane gas the man emitted, which caused a flare-up that set his genitals on fire. "When I woke up, my penis and scrotum were burning like hell," the man told the Danish newspaper *BT.* The surgeon was quoted as saying, "No one considered the possibility the man would break wind during the operation, let alone that it would catch fire. It was an unfortunate accident." The man is suing for pain and suffering.

The United Kingdom Central Council of Nursing, Midwifery and Health **warned British nurses to refrain from using derogatory abbreviations** in their notes (which are included in the patient's medical records). Some of the offensive abbreviations are: FLK (Funny-Looking Kid), PIN (Pain in the Neck), and BUNDY (But Unfortunately Not Dead Yet).

Chart Toppers

Even more actual doctors' notes.

- By the time he was admitted, his rapid heart had stopped, and he was feeling better.

- Patient has chest pain if she lies on her left side for over a year.

- On the second day the knee was better and on the third day it had completely disappeared.

- She has had no rigors or shaking chills, but her husband states she was very hot in bed last night.

- She slipped on the ice and apparently her legs went in separate directions in early December.

- The penicillin causes dizziness and shortness of breasts.

The grand opening of the $20 million Indian Health Service hospital in Pine Ridge, South Dakota, was delayed three months when **officials realized they had forgotten to plan for and install a telephone system** in the building.

If It Itches—Scratch It

A Swedish woman from Stockholm had an itch that she just couldn't reach. The itch was in the back of her throat, and it was so irritating that she had to do something. So she grabbed a toothbrush, and "The brush simply disappeared down my throat," she said. The woman went to the hospital after having difficulty breathing, and doctors were able to remove the toothbrush with a remote-controlled miniature grip. She was released from the hospital twenty hours after being admitted and was sent home—toothbrush in hand this time.

At the other end of the spectrum, a man from Great Britain used a toothbrush to soothe an itch, but the opening he stuck his brush into wasn't his mouth. **Doctors removed the toothbrush from the man's rectum,** where it had worked its way deep inside, near his pelvis. I just wonder if he asked for the toothbrush back, as the lady in the previous story did.

Dangerous
Idiots

The Fur Is Flying

Two janitors working at a Ceres, California, school were hospitalized and sixteen pupils injured in a failed attempt by the janitors to kill a gopher. After catching the gopher, the two janitors decided the best way to kill it would be by pouring a gum- and wax-removing compound on it, and they did. After the ordeal, one of the janitors needed a break and lit a cigarette. Bad move. The gopher exploded, causing injuries to the janitors and students and, of course, the gopher.

In order to prove his supernatural powers, a hermit living outside Caracas, Venezuela, **bet his neighbors that he could hypnotize a jaguar.** He lost both the bet and his left arm.

Hey, Idiot!

Next Time, Shout It Out!

A man living in Clermont, France, took the expression "cleaning house" to a whole new level. Gerard Ropuille told police that he was trying to remove a stubborn grease stain from his shirt when the accident occurred. He confessed that he placed the shirt in his washing machine, and then added a cup of gasoline in hopes of removing that pesky stain. When the washing machine changed cycles, a spark ignited the gasoline and blew out the first floor of Ropuille's home, knocking him unconscious at the same time. Ropuille made the "duh" statement of the year after the accident by saying, "I feel a bit stupid." I couldn't have said it better myself.

All in the family: A police officer from East Haddam, Connecticut, was on patrol when a woman swerved into his lane. He pulled the woman over and was writing her up for DUI when her husband, who was leading her home, pulled up alongside the officer. **The husband was also arrested for DUI.**

Sign, Sign, Everywhere a Sign

A billboard in Scranton, Pennsylvania, announced, "Bring in this ad and you'll get a free pair of shoes." Well, three very literal people did just that. They tore down the fourteen-by-forty-eight-foot sign and lugged it into the Shoestrings boutique. After some "discussion" and the look of shock left their faces, the owners of the boutique honored the massive coupon and gave the three free pairs of shoes. I'm just thankful it wasn't a double coupon.

A hunter in Tehran, Iran, jumped into a snake pit armed with a shotgun and quickly pinned a serpent to the ground with the butt of his 12 gauge. The snake coiled around the trigger, causing the weapon to fire. **Only the snake made it out of the pit alive.**

Hey, Idiot!

Up, Up, and Away

Union rules are pretty tough and must be adhered to, especially in the high-pressure world of air traffic controllers. Rules stipulate that air traffic controllers must take one break every two hours, and it was time for this air traffic controller's break. So she pushed herself away from the radar screen at the control tower in Benbecula in the Western Isles of Scotland and left for a thirty-minute lunch. The only problem was that because of a shortage of air traffic controllers there was only one person "pushing tin" that day. Her radar screen wasn't the only thing she left—there was also a plane carrying fifty-five passengers circling the airport, waiting for landing instructions. When the passengers and their families discovered the reason for the thirty-minute delay, I'm sure their lawyers were in the full, upright, and locked position.

A scorned woman in Hong Kong, upset that her boyfriend was planning to return to his wife, **doused both herself and him in paint thinner** and threatened to strike a match. The man sweet-talked the woman into giving him the match and then, to calm his nerves, he used it to light a cigarette. He survived, she didn't.

A Second Time Around

Icelandic police noticed a car weaving erratically and pulled the driver over. While they were writing him up, they noticed that he looked very familiar. Was he someone they knew from school; was he someone wanted on an outstanding warrant? No, they realized he was the same man they had stopped for drunk driving ninety minutes earlier and had allowed to go home in a taxi. The reason they didn't recognize him sooner was that he was now driving a different car. After another trip to the police station, authorities decided to let the man go home again and called another cab. Maybe he wanted one more for the road and needed more road to go.

A man in Jerusalem was arrested for driving down the road at a high rate of speed **using his elbows to steer the car** as he spoke into mobile phones he was holding in both hands.

Going Off Half-Cocked

The police department was conducting a special training for its police officers at the firing range at Lorton Correctional Facility in Lorton, Virginia. The officers were required to lie on their backs and fire fully automatic weapons into the air at special targets. Unfortunately, the firing range was designed for short-range weapons like shotguns. Twelve houses and three cars in a local neighborhood were riddled with stray bullets. Chief Charles Ramsey closed the range permanently after determining that "open-air live-fire ranges and populated residential areas simply do not mix." Sounds like someone was shooting blanks, doesn't it?

An elderly Stratford, Connecticut, man was hospitalized **when he attempted to create an additional belt hole** using a pointy-nosed bullet as the punch.

Chicken of the Sea

An unidentified fisherman was rushed to the hospital suffering from broken vertebrae and a concussion. Apparently he and another fisherman got into an argument while sorting fish after a successful haul, and the other fisherman attacked him with a twenty-pound tuna. Sorry, Charlie.

A husband and wife in Huntsville, Alabama, were **hospitalized with severe burns** after trying to loosen the dried paint in several cans of aerosol paint by heating them on the stove.

Knock Your Block Off

A Spring Hill, Tennessee, man was so frustrated after his car died on him again that he killed the motor—literally. Motorists were surprised and frightened when they saw the man firing an AK-47 assault rifle into his 1988 Oldsmobile. "I understand he unloaded three thirty-round clips into the vehicle," Sheriff Enoch George said. That gives a whole new meaning to the phrase "gunning the engine."

An auto mechanic from Alamo, Michigan, couldn't locate a mysterious rattle in a truck left with him for service. Unbelievably, he asked a friend to drive while he hung underneath the truck to locate the source of the noise. Unfortunately, the mechanic's clothes got wound around the drive shaft. **The knock is still around but the mechanic isn't.**

Hey, Idiot!

Darwin Was Right

A Little Rock, Arkansas, man couldn't figure out exactly how much gas was left in the bottom of the gas can because he couldn't see the bottom of the container. In a cliché come to life, he pulled out his cigarette lighter to find out. The thirty-year-old threw the can down once the fumes caught fire but was unable to contain the resulting inferno that injured a friend and burned down his trailer. The accidental arsonist suffered only minor burns to his hands—and a burning sensation that he's a real moron.

An excited eighteen-year-old girl was driving with her mother on their way to the girl's first driving test in Euclid, Florida. The test was canceled because she took a wrong turn and **crashed the car through the front window of the Euclid Post Office**, injuring one customer.

Hey, Idiot!

Solar-Powered

In the hopes of getting a better view during a solar eclipse, a twenty-four-year-old German man climbed a power pylon and awaited the awesome event. In order to steady himself for the spectacle he was about to observe, he reached out and grabbed a twenty-thousand-volt electric cable. Fortunately, it wasn't lights out for the sun worshiper, as he suffered only severe burns.

Eleven members of the same Rio de Janeiro family were rushed to a hospital suffering from food poisoning after eating a traditional Brazilian meal with a little something extra—arsenic. The woman who prepared the meal thought that she had simply added a dash of cumin, not knowing that **her mother-in-law had recently purchased rat poison** and for some reason had decided to store it in an herb jar near the rest of the spices.

You're Known by the Company You Keep

In the spirit of "love thy neighbor," two men living next door to each other decided to split the cost of yardwork and purchased a brand-new Black & Decker gas-powered lawn mower together. Warmed by the glow of neighborly love, they decided it would be a great idea to use the lawn mower to trim the hedges that divided their property. So with one neighbor on his side of the hedge and the other neighbor on his, they hoisted the lawn mower into the air and glided it across the top of the hedge. The mower blade snagged on the shrub and the resulting kickback caused serious injury to both men. Again working in tandem, both men decided to sue the manufacturer on the grounds that there was no warning on the lawn mower stating that it shouldn't be used as a hedge trimmer.

A Canadian officer arrested a driver he noticed speeding down the highway and swerving erratically. **It took the woman driver several minutes to notice the officer** motioning her to pull over because she was in the middle of reading a book.

What Goes Up...

One hunter in Milledgeville, Georgia, had chased a raccoon into a tree so that his partner could get a clear shot at it with his rifle. Once the animal was treed, the other hunter fired, killing the animal. While the two gave each other the thumbs-up to celebrate their superior intellect over the stupid animal, the stupid and dead raccoon plummeted sixty feet from its perch and landed directly on the hunter, knocking him out cold and breaking three of his vertebrae.

Two teenage cousins in Plymouth, Wisconsin, were curious about **what it would feel like to be shot.** A thirty-four-year-old relative stopped the two from shooting each other by offering to do it for them. Both boys were hospitalized and treated for gunshot wounds to the leg—the older man was arrested.

A Real Stink Bomb

Several teenage pranksters thought it would be funny to put a homemade pipe bomb in a portable toilet at a construction site in Manchester Township, Pennsylvania. After placing the bomb, the boys ran off a safe distance to watch the fireworks. They waited and waited—nothing happened. One of the boys decided to find out what happened to the bomb and went back to the Porta-John to investigate. Curiosity, or was it stupidity, got the best of the boy, and he picked up the bomb to examine it. The resulting explosion alerted the police, who soon arrested two of the boys and took the mad bomber to the hospital. I guess being in a toilet is as good a place as any when you get the crap blown out of you.

A Wisconsin man wanting a cigarette reached for his cigarette lighter but **mistakenly grabbed his .25-caliber semi-automatic pistol.** Instead of firing up a smoke, he shot a hole through his hand and wounded his friend in the thigh.

Hey, Idiot!

Hunter-Gatherer

While hunting in Florida's Ocala National Forest, a man came across an endangered species, or should I say a dangerous species—a World War II–era bomb. The man, obviously looking for another trophy for his den, decided to take the bomb home, and he loaded it into his pickup truck. He took the bomb back to camp, and when the other hunters saw what he had bagged, they called the police. The military jumped into action, and fifty people were evacuated while they retrieved the outdated, but very dangerous explosive. Looking back on his big-game adventures, the hunter remarked, "Common sense should have kicked in a little better." Now we know how certain species become extinct.

Police in Warsaw, Poland, trying to capture an escaped circus tiger **accidentally shot and killed the veterinarian** trying to tranquilize it.

Paging Doctors Howard and Fine

A plastic surgeon in Boxford, Massachusetts, had rented a backhoe in order to do some serious work in his yard. After digging deep into the ground he noticed a "strong smell" of rotten eggs and thought he might have ruptured a gas main. Immediately he called the gas company. "The house exploded as he was making the call," said a gas company spokesman. "He said, 'Forget it. The house is gone.'" The plastic surgeon's half-million-dollar, five-bedroom house was completely destroyed by the explosion. The doctor had failed to call the gas company to see if there were any underground lines before he'd started digging. Well, he had an excuse—he was a plastic surgeon, not a brain surgeon.

A British tourist **didn't think anyone would believe his fish story** so he brought the catch back to the hotel with him and placed it in the bathtub: a five-foot-long live shark.

Drain Cleaner or Brain Cleaner

A man from Adel, Georgia, filed a lawsuit against the maker of Liquid Fire drain cleaner alleging that the dangerous material leaked out of his homemade container, spilled on his legs, and caused "extensive, excruciating burns and destruction of flesh." Liquid Fire actually comes in its own spillproof container, which the man apparently thought looked too flimsy, so he poured the contents into his own container (which is where the leak occurred). So why did he sue the makers of Liquid Fire? He claims the company is at fault for his stupid mistake because the original package somehow created the impression that it lacked sturdiness and that forced the man to pour it into another container. Is it just me or does it seem like his brain is in a flimsy container, too?

A young man had his arm broken because he was walking too close to the train tracks and **a passing train knocked the surfboard out of his hands.**

Stop Bugging Me!

A Los Angeles woman with bug problems thought she would use a fogger-style "bug bomb" to eliminate the pests. She must have thought to herself, "I have so many bugs that I'll need more than one to get rid of them all," so she used thirty of them at the same time. True to the name "bug bomb," once these thirty foggers were activated in every room in her house, including the kitchen, a spark ignited the fumes, shattered the windows, burned the woman (who stayed in the house during the fumigation for some reason), and raised the roof three inches. All eight hundred square feet of her home suffered $30,000 in damages. No word on how the bugs made out.

A twenty-five-year-old woman in Mount Prospect, Illinois, lost the toes on her right foot when **she decided to crawl under a slow-moving train** as a shortcut to the correct platform.

A Real Mobile Home

An Amtrak train loaded with sports fans was hurtling down the tracks in Washington when the conductor looked up and noticed there was something on the tracks—a house! The train smashed into the house, tearing it to small pieces, but fortunately, no one was hurt. Moments before the crash, two men were seen on the roof of the house holding up electric wires so they could move it across the tracks. Here's the first example of a house on both sides of the tracks.

A man from Winnipeg, Canada, purchased a military-style bulletproof vest and wanted to try it out. **He asked a friend to shoot him in the chest** with a .22-caliber rifle—the vest passed the test. The man then stuffed a phone book under the vest and asked his friend to shoot him with a 12-gauge shotgun. The man survived but suffered cracked ribs. Police have asked the court to withhold gun ownership privileges for the pair for the next five years.

That's Why Some People Spell It Do*nut*

Not satisfied with the snacks provided at a party at the Ferstl Palace in Vienna, a young partygoer started rummaging through the kitchen to find something he wanted. He looked in the freezer and found a frozen doughnut that looked like it would hit the spot. The man couldn't find a microwave so he took the frozen pastry out to the living room and held it over a candle to thaw it out. During the heating process, things quickly got out of hand, and the fire spread to a nearby sofa and then caught the wood paneling on fire. Some six hundred guests were evacuated from the building. The man suffered slight burns from his attempt to put out the fire before it could spread further. The doughnut was a complete loss. Thank God it wasn't an éclair!

In a cliché come to life, a nineteen-year-old Indiana man **couldn't figure out why his gun was jammed** and wouldn't fire. So, that's right, he looked down the barrel to find the source of the problem. He soon discovered the gun was working perfectly after it shot a hole in his face.

A Pocket Full of Trouble

A man in Tallahassee, Florida, was relieving himself in public when a passing police officer noticed and yelled at him to stop. The man, who was smoking a cigarette at the time, put the still burning butt into his pocket, zipped up his pants, and ran away. The police officer gave chase. Things started heating up—literally. I suppose the man didn't realize that fires love oxygen, and his running was fueling the cigarette in his pocket. Soon the police officer noticed billowing smoke coming from the man's pants and continued to yell for him to stop—or maybe stop, drop, and roll. The man discovered the fire and quickly unloosed his belt but never stopped running until the trousers slipped to his ankles, causing him to fall. The officer had to call for reinforcements as the man punched and kicked at him when he tried to extinguish the flames. Another officer arrived, tore off the man's still burning trousers, and placed him under arrest. I'm sure there were a lot of jokes in the precinct that night about "hot pants."

A twenty-one-year-old Welsh tourist was sent to the hospital after **he fell from the back of a bus while mooning passing motorists.**

The Big Bang Theory

A construction worker in Shanghai, China, identified only as Zhang, didn't believe for some reason that the explosives used by the construction industry were particularly powerful. Zhang made a bet with his friend that he would sit on a basket on top of a stone and have his friend place several detonators under the stone and light them. His friend took him up on the bet, and in the resulting explosion, "the stone plate, the basket, and his rear end all went up in smoke," according to press accounts. Doctors say it will be "some time" before Zhang will be able to walk normally.

To commemorate the hundred-year anniversary of eliminating the plague, citizens of Yenshui, Taiwan, held a celebration with fireworks. They lined up wearing protective, bulky clothing and **had people fire bottle rockets directly at them.** The villagers believed that being hit by the small exploding missiles would bring them good luck. Unfortunately, thirty apparently very lucky people suffered serious injuries when the rockets got tangled up in their bulky clothing before exploding.

Idiotic Inventions

Hey, Idiot!

If You Can Make It There You'll Make It Anywhere...

Tired of reading on the john? Or maybe you forgot your radio and want to while away the time with a little music. Inventor Roger Weisskopf has just the thing for you. He demonstrated his latest creation at the annual Geneva (Switzerland) Invention Exhibition: a singing toilet seat. The toilet seat features a picture of Louis Armstrong and plays the song "New York, New York" when sat upon. I don't know about you, but I don't care to hear the words "Start spreading the news" as soon as my bottom hits the john.

— — — — — — — — —

This "phone" has way too many shortcomings for us to consider it as a serious way of communicating. The unit is worthless to us.

—Internal memo, Western Union, 1876

Hey, Idiot!

Turning a Deaf Ear

Lino Missio, an Italian physics student, devised a condom that plays a selection of Beethoven if it breaks during use. The inventor announced that the condom is coated with a substance that, when ruptured, changes electrical conductivity and sets off a microchip to produce the music. Missio, who now owns a patent on the conductive conducting condom, said he might replace the music with a verbal warning, which would alert wearers if the condom breaks during use. But if the condom is being used correctly—how is anyone going to hear a thing?

Two inventors from Fremont, California, obtained a patent for a golf club that is designed to fire a golf ball up to 250 yards. **The club is fitted with an explosive charge** in the head that detonates upon contact with the ball.

Hey, Idiot!

Smoking Is Not Allowed

Pu Danming, a Chinese inventor, claims to have had great success marketing the "healthy cigarettes" that he introduced in Beijing. The cigarette is actually a hollow tube containing Chinese herbs, a small battery, a microchip, and several other items, but no tobacco whatsoever. In fact, you don't even light Danming's cigarette. However, when the smoker takes a puff, it activates the battery, which powers a small light at the tip of the cigarette, giving the appearance of fire. The smoker inhales the aroma of the Chinese herbs, which Danming claims are also good against cancer. To top it all off, when the smoker takes a draw of the cigarette, a patriotic song is played. And you thought Kent and its Micronite filter was cool!

Bernd Helbig, a tavern owner from Halle, Germany, invented and introduced **"beersicles,"** which sell for about $3.50 each. And "beersicles" are just want you think they are.

Hey, Idiot!

Pay No Attention to the Noise Inside My Head

There's interactive television, interactive Web sites, interactive theater—and now there's interactive candy. First there was Spin Pops, the battery-operated candy that spins, then Pez came out with the motorized Pez dispenser (why, we're not sure). And now another company has come out with "Sound Bites," the world's first interactive candy. The candy is connected to a microchip inside the stick that plays music, cartoon clips, and sound effects, and can only be heard by the sucker (or is it suckee?). Anyway, the music travels through the candy and is heard, thanks to "advanced technology," because it transmits vibrations through the teeth into the middle ear. Now, thanks to some wise inventor, we have a candy that rots not only the teeth but also the mind.

Edwin Shoemaker, the man who invented the La-Z-Boy recliner, **was found dead** in his Monroe, Michigan, home on March 15, 1999—in a La-Z-Boy recliner.

Stand Back—It's on Spin!

Usually when one comes in contact with human waste (you know what I'm talking about), they want to wash not only their hands but also their clothes. However, Japanese inventor Nishi Ishizaki created a different take on this basic human response. He has invented a washing machine that runs on human waste (excrement, in particular). The machine traps methane gas from the waste and uses it to power an electrical generator. Ishizaki claims that twenty pounds of human manure is sufficient to do five loads of laundry (that's on a load-to-load ratio). But what has the inventor done about the natural smell of excrement? Nothing. That's the biggest drawback of his invention—it stinks. Ishizaki admits the smell is a problem but he realizes that once he's figured out a way to make the washing machine smell-free, he'll make a small fortune with campers and people without electricity. Just in case you're wondering where one might find twenty pounds of human poop at a time, don't worry; the inventor explains that cat and dog droppings can be used, too.

An inventor created **gas-filled furniture** that is designed to float up to the ceiling when not in use, to give more space.

Hey, Idiot!

Poopsicle

In case you're interested in Mr. Ishizaki's poop-powered washing machine, you might want to pick up a couple of cans of "Clear-up." "Clear-up" is a new product from a British inventor that "is an aerosol spray that freezes any horrible, messy dog doo and transforms it into a solid, hard lump that can be easily picked up," said Nick Westcott, managing director of the Animal Health Co., Ltd. The spray sells for only $5.72. "Dog wardens are raving about it. It's transformed their lives," said Westcott. If freezing dog poop has transformed someone's life—I wonder what their life was beforehand.

An **automatic bingo machine** was invented by a Hollister, California, man whose name is—Wilson Q. Invencion.

Is the D-Cup Half Full or Half Empty?

The Triumph Company of Japan introduced its "Body-Warmth Bra Two-Cup Ozeki." It's a standard brassiere that contains a waterproof pocket designed to be filled expressly with the popular rice wine sake. Sake is best served slightly warm and once inserted into the "Body-Warmth Bra Two-Cup Ozeki" will heat to body temperature in about an hour. I guess it's great for those two-fisted drinkers.

Let's Give Him a Hand

Albert Cohen of Troy, New York, received a patent for a device that will surely be a hit with the lonely sports fan. He designed an artificial arm that is constructed to be attached to a wall, a desk, or the floor. Why? Because when the sports fan's favorite team makes a great play and there's no one there to give the solo sports fan a high-five, then, you guessed it, the person can give a high-five to the artificial hand. I guess the artificial hand could also be used to hold an extra beer, too.

Smoke Gets in Your Eyes—
But No One Else's

Now that rabid nonsmoking policies have popped up everywhere, what's a smoker to do so he or she can enjoy a smoke
and not offend anyone else? Well, engineer Wal Netschert
hopes he has the answer. Netschert has created a smokers' hat
with a facial shield that he claims completely filters the noxious
elements out of cigarette smoke before they are released into the
environment. The apparatus fits on the user's forehead and
contains a series of filters (measuring about 6 inches square
by 3 inches high). A facial shield is positioned to capture any
drifting smoke from the cigarette itself. Netschert has been
a smoker for forty years and says he will continue to smoke
because it calms his nerves. The catalysts for the invention,
Netschert admits, are the militant nonsmokers, whom he
refers to as "FAFs—Fresh Air Freaks."

The **"Tootsie Tube"**—a pipe that catches a person's breath
and funnels it down the bed to keep his or her toes warm.

Gas Wars

Another invention that's ripe for sports fans—or any fan of beans and broccoli—has been introduced by a firm called Ultra Tech Products of Houston, Texas. The company is offering the TooT TrappeR Chair Cushion and it does just what you'd think it does. The product is a foam cushion with a "superactivated carbon filter" that traps and filters offensive body gases before they escape. Do you think the TooT TrappeR will ever become a household staple? I wouldn't hold my breath.

The Golden Retriever

Sports Illustrated reported on a Houston, Texas, man who invented a device perfect for those lazy afternoon golfers—or those lazy people who golf in the afternoon. The patented contraption is described as a cup that goes inside a golf hole and, when a ball is knocked into the hole, periscopes up so that the golfer doesn't have to bend down to pick up the ball. So much for the excuse that people golf for the exercise.

Hey, Idiot!

This Little Piggy Went to Market

Sick and tired of unsightly toe jam? Constantly berated at work and humiliated because of your chronic filthy toes? Need to rid yourself of toe jam once and for all without the bother of stooping over? Well, here is Ronald M. Hannon to the rescue. Hannon has recently invented and is currently marketing Toe Floss. Designed to clean between the toes without the user bending over, Toe Floss is a three-foot-long rope that attaches to the shower floor and, when held taut, allows users to scrub between their toes. There are a few other areas on the human body that could use flossing—but I'll leave that up to another inventor.

Overijse, Belgium, horticulturalist Luc Mertes introduced a line of **skirts and dresses made of live grass.** The grass will continue to grow as long as the material stays damp.

Under Where?

An invention from Japan is sure to be a hit with the more modest Japanese women. Keiko Yoshida, a Tokyo fabrics worker, announced that she had invented women's underwear that automatically shreds itself in extremely hot water. Yoshida created the underwear because of government regulations requiring all garbage to be packaged in transparent bags. She believes a lot of Japanese women would rather have their old underwear dissolved than seen by passersby. Now that this underwear is on the market, I wonder if warm water contests will take the place of wet T-shirt contests.

In the future computers will probably not weigh any more than 1.5 ton.

—Popular Mechanics, *1949*

Hey, Idiot!

http://www.surf&turf.com

What can you do with the eight minutes it takes for your Veal Parmigiana to cook in the microwave? How about surf the Net, do a little on-line banking, or drop into your favorite chat room (and maybe pick up a few new recipes while you're at it)? The people who want to combine microwave cooking and the Internet are just the market that American developers NCR are hoping to attract with their combination microwave-computer. It really is both a microwave and a computer designed to access the Internet (it has a color monitor instead of a glass door). Aside from being a strange idea, there are a few problems with the new technology: one is wave interference. Microwaves and computer electronics are two of the most incompatible things around; the microwaves tend to scramble the sensitive computer chips. NCR hasn't figured out a way to shield the electronics from the microwaves, nor have they figured out a way to jam all that technology into a convenient size, but they are sure they'll soon have a hit on their hands. Standing with your face close to a computer monitor is one thing—how about asking people to stand with their face close to a microwave?

Thomas Edison was **afraid of the dark.**

Bear-Fisted Fighting

Troy Hurtubise, a scrap-metal dealer from North Bay, Ontario, didn't do so well in his first encounter with a grizzly bear in 1984. That chance meeting put him on a ten-year quest to create the perfect suit of armor—one in which you can successfully wrestle a grizzly bear. Hurtubise's tenacity won him the "Ig Nobel" award, a Harvard-based spoof award presented to people whose achievements "cannot or should not be reproduced." Hurtubise was the proud recipient of the "safety engineering" award. "He's a classic inventor," said Marc Abrahams, editor of the journal that assists in presenting the awards, the satirical *Annals of Improbable Research,* based in Cambridge, Massachusetts. "He gets this idea and he really sticks with it." Hurtubise spent nearly ten years developing the suit at a personal cost of more than $100,000 (he had to file for bankruptcy)—and during all that time he couldn't find a bear to wrestle.

Janet Merel of Deerfield, Illinois, introduced Diet Dirt, which **sells for $10 a bag.** It is sterilized soil that you can sprinkle on your favorite foods to make them taste horrible, making you want to eat less and thereby causing you to lose weight.

Hey, Idiot!

Staff Artist

A body-paint artist revealed his design for a skintight latex condom—which is painted onto the penis—in a trade fair in Vienna, Austria. He plans to market bottles with enough paint for three applications for about $8.00. The main problem with the product, however, is that there is a seven-minute wait time while the paint dries. This isn't something you'd give to a temperamental artist—remember what happened to van Gogh.

Rub-a-Dub-Dub

Irish inventor Mark Bradley created a unique triangular wedge designed to be placed in the middle of one's bathtub in order to reduce the amount of water needed to fill the tub. But wait, there's more! When not used as a bath-water budgeter, this handsomely designed, handcrafted wonder can also serve as a table for books or a very large pool rack.

How Do You Like Your Ribs?

Carjackings have become so rampant in South Africa that people are now afraid to drive their cars. Inventor Charles Fourie grew tired of living in a victimized society and decided to create something that would make carjackers "toast." Fourie created the "Blaster," a device that mounts under a car. Does it blast loud noise if a suspected carjacker approaches? No. Does it blast a verbal warning? No. The "Blaster" is connected to a foot pedal inside the car, and when the car's owner feels threatened all he or she has to do is depress the pedal, activating flamethrowers located on both sides of the car. *Voilà*! A crispy carjacker carcass. Fourie has already installed twenty-five "Blasters," which have been deemed legal by Johannesburg Police Superintendent David Walkley. Walkley isn't just a supporter of the "Blaster"—he's also a proud owner of one. Now the term *jump in your car and fire it up* has a whole new meaning.

Get a grip! British doctor R. John Nicholls and his team of researchers have developed **just the thing** for people who suffer from fecal incontinence—an artificial bowel sphincter.

Idiots in Education

Testing Our Patients

The following are verbatim quotes from eighth-grade exams:

When you breath, you inspire. When you do not breath, you expire.

H_2O is hot water, and CO_2 is cold water.

When you smell an odorless gas, it is probably carbon monoxide.

Three kinds of blood vessels are arteries, vanes, and caterpillars.

The moon is a planet just like earth, only it is even deader.

And finally . . .

Artificial insemination is when the farmer does it to the cow instead of the bull.

A West Virginia schoolteacher was **ordered to undergo psychiatric evaluation** after reporting her toddler son missing. The report triggered a massive manhunt that was eventually called off when the woman remembered that she had dropped the boy off at day care as she does every workday.

Hey, Idiot!

Drawing Your Name out of a Hat

A group of female students at the College Park campus of the University of Maryland randomly chose several male students' names from the student telephone directory and printed up flyers. The eighty-six flyers, which the nine girls tacked up around campus, read: NOTICE: THESE MEN ARE POTENTIAL RAPISTS. The girls claimed they were trying to increase awareness of sexual abuse of women, but many of the male students were angry over their actions. Said one female student, defending what she and her classmates had done, "I don't think we've done anything wrong. The word 'potential' was used. That's not accusatory at all." This girl is a potential idiot—that, or a future lawyer.

Two fifth graders were ordered by a judge not to socialize with each other again after their make-believe marriage ended in make-believe divorce. The family of the eleven-year-old girl filed a complaint, alleging threats and abuse from the ten-year-old ex-pretend-husband. The two were **"married"** on the school playground by a ten-year-old make-believe **"minister."**

Notes fro...

These are actual excuse notes... spelling) collected by Nisheeth Par... Medical Branch at Galveston:

My son is under a doctor's care and should no... today. Please execute him.

Please excuse Lisa for being absent. She was sick and I had her shot.

Dear School: Please ekscuse John being absent on Jan. 28, 29, 30, 31, 32, and also 33.

Please excuse Gloria from Jim today. She is administrating.

Please excuse Roland from P.E. for a few days. Yesterday he fell out of a tree and misplaced his hip.

John has been absent because he had two teeth taken out of his face.

Carlos was absent yesterday because he was playing football. He was hurt in the growing part.

At a sex-education rally in a Chicago high school, an abstinence advocate told the teenagers that if they feel a sexual urge coming on, **"Just eat a Snickers bar. You'll be fine!"**

Idiot!

Fill in the Blank Council

ng an annual convention of the National Council of chers of English, some members suggested eliminating the ord "English" from the title of their organization because they taught not only English but also a variety of languages. Another group wanted to drop "National" because the word appeals to nationalism. Still another group wanted "Teachers" dropped because they wanted to be known by more PC terms like "facilitators" or "guides." Apparently there were no objections to "Council of." But let's just wait until their next meeting.

— — — — — — — — — —

```
In Friday's Daily Athenaeum, it was
incorrectly reported that Gabrielle
   St. Leger, a candidate for WVU
[West Virginia University] Homecoming
   Queen, said that she had "done a
 lot of this university." St. Leger
  actually said that she had "done a
      lot for this university."
```

—*West Virginia University's student newspaper, October 25, 2000.*

The Ivory Arches

A woman candidate for the school board in Holly Hill, Florida, claimed in her campaign that she held a bachelor's degree in business administration from Hamburger University. That's right, Hamburger University, not Hamburg. When pressed for details, the woman explained that it was an extensive training course offered by McDonald's. Officials from McDonald's said they do not offer such a degree but added, "We offer a bachelor of hamburgerology at the end of an eleven-day course in advanced operations." The woman defended her actions and said, "It does say on my diploma that it is a degree in bachelor." Later, as the woman was walking home, she was detained and interrogated by Mayor McCheese.

A dozen students sued Southern Methodist University seeking unspecified damages because a computer course was too hard, and **all twelve students in the class failed.** University officials offered the twelve disciples a chance to repeat the course, but the group wants its money back. Some students claiming to have taken time from work to attend the class are seeking further compensation.

Hey, Idiot!

A Third of the Way There

A superior court judge in Danbury, Connecticut, ruled in favor of a middle school teacher who filed for reinstatement on the grounds that she was wrongfully dismissed. The woman taught English, Social Studies, and Business and was ruled incompetent to teach in two of those three subjects (English and Social Studies). The judge ruled that since the woman wasn't deemed incompetent in Business, however, she would have to be rehired to teach that course. Well, like they say, two out of three ain't bad.

Reacting to school vandalism and a downtown shooting, officials at Round Rock High School in Texas banned the color red on Friday. Apparently the gang responsible for these incidents wore red—**about forty students wearing red items were sequestered in the library,** and their parents were called. The American Civil Liberties Union remarked that it was the first known case of a school reacting to gang fears by banning a complete primary color.

Who Knows What Evil Lurks in the Hearts of Men

The Assistant Dean of Student Life at Vassar College commented on hearing that several male students were found innocent of rape charges: "Men who are unjustly accused of rape can sometimes gain from the experience." She elaborated, "They have a lot of pain, but it is not a pain that I would necessarily have spared them. I think it ideally initiates a process of self-exploration. 'How do I see women?' 'If I did not violate her, could I have?' 'Do I have the potential to do what they say I did?' These are good questions." A prime example of being held guilty after being proven innocent.

According to an article in the *New York Times,* **a professor at Boston University was caught plagiarizing** entire passages for a speech based on an article that, itself, had been plagiarized, in part, from a story that had been printed in the *Boston Globe.* The subject of the professor's speech—journalistic incompetence.

Hey, Idiot!

More Notes from Home

Megan could not come to school today because she has been bothered by very close veins.

Chris will not be in school cus he has an acre in his side.

Please excuse Ray Friday from school. He has very loose vowels.

Please excuse Tommy for being absent yesterday. He had diarrhea and his boots leak.

Irving was absent yesterday because he missed his bust.

Please excuse Jimmy for being. It was his father's fault.

Please excuse Jennifer for missing school yesterday. We forgot to get the Sunday paper off the porch, and when we found it Monday, we thought it was Sunday.

Sally won't be in school a week from Friday. We have to attend her funeral.

A thirteen-year-old Portland, Oregon, student was suspended for a week because he violated the school's zero-tolerance policy on alcohol. The boy was caught swallowing some Scope mouthwash because, he said, **"The lunch kind of tasted bad, I didn't have any place to spit."**

Making an Example out of Yourself

A law professor at George Mason University was trying to make a point to his class about how certain hurtful words might prompt legal action. His first-year torts class listened as the professor created a hypothetical situation involving the KKK carrying signs that read KILL THE NIGGERS through a predominantly black neighborhood. How easy was it for someone to file a complaint and possibly a lawsuit? the professor questioned. Very easy, came the answer, as students were soon circulating a petition denouncing the professor's insensitivity, calling for an immediate apology, and demanding that the word "Nigger" be banned from classrooms. Case closed.

A concerned parent, realizing his son was in danger of failing the seventh grade, jumped into action. He tutored the thirteen-year-old student from Harrold Middle School in Pittsburgh **two hours a day for eleven weeks.** What was the result? The boy finished with an 85.5 average, and his father was arrested for removing his son from study hall.

Why Johnny Can't Read

An article appearing in the *Miami Herald* was highly critical of the Dade County School Board. The author of the article, who was also the cosponsor of a school choice bill in Florida, received hundreds of angry letters from students. It is highly likely, however, that the students were coached by their teachers to write the letters and that the students themselves didn't fully understand the subject on which they were writing. Here are some excerpts from letters received by the article's author, accidentally making his case about the poor quality of education in Miami.

- "You will regrate stopping all this stuff like summer school while I don't really care if you stop summer school because should not have to go to school in are summer. It is are time but we need are education."

- "I think the budget is getting worse so put down the big company with higher money. little company lower value and keep the school for cutting teacher out their job."

An associate professor at the University of Manitoba, Canada, **has spent the last eight years** fighting a ticket for running a "Stop" sign. His argument is that the word "stop" is too vague.

Which Is Witch?

A vice principal at Panorama Middle School in Colorado Springs, Colorado, lectured and reprimanded eight twelve-year-old girls for nearly two hours "on the evils of witchcraft" in response to accusations that the girls were "casting spells" on classmates. "We had received concerns from students and parents," announced the school's principal, "[who] said that [the sixth-grade girls] were going to cast a spell on them. And they were reading books about witchcraft." When confronted with the last accusation the girls admitted they were reading a book about witches, *Salem's Trial,* that they had checked out of the school library.

Your job is not to judge the rightness and wrongness of each student's answer. Let those determinations come from the class.

—*A California guide to the teaching of mathematics*

Hey, Idiot!

A Damn Stern Punishment

The Hendersonville (Tennessee) High School student handbook has the harshest punishment for the use of profanity of any high school in the world. The handbook reads: "Profane language will not be tolerated. Stern discipline will be death to any student guilty of this conduct." Wow, talk about your zero tolerance. The principal of the school, however, explained that the word "death" was mistakenly put in for the word "dealt." "Most folks know that it was a misprint," said the principal. I hope to hell it . . . ahhhhhhhhhhhhhh . . .

The *Sunday Telegraph* reported that the **British government approved a new test** that gives credit to students for getting their names, the names of their schools, and the date correct. In the math section, sixteen-year-old students are shown five pencils and need to respond with the correct number of pencils as well as identifying the longest one.

I Didn't Know That Was Going to Be on the Test

The following are examples of answers to "History" questions gathered by teachers from eighth grade through college.

- The First World War, cause by the assignation of the Arch-Duck by a surf, ushered in a new error in the annals of human history.

- Gravity was invented by Issac Walton. It is chiefly noticeable in the Autumn, when the apples are falling off the trees.

- On the night of April 14, 1865, Lincoln went to the theater and got shot in his seat by one of the actors in a moving picture show. The believed assassinator was John Wilkes Booth, a supposedly insane actor. This ruined Booth's career.

- George Washington married Martha Curtis and in due time became the Father of Our Country. The Constitution of the United States was adopted to secure domestic hostility. Under the Constitution the people enjoyed the right to keep bare arms.

- One of the causes of the Revolutionary Wars was the English put tacks in their tea.

- Writing at the same time as Shakespeare was Miquel Cervantes. He wrote "Donkey Hote." The next great author was John Milton. Milton wrote "Paradise Lost." Then his wife died and he wrote "Paradise Regained."

Hey, Idiot!

My Teacher's the Bomb!

It was a tense moment at the Lindsay Thurber High School in Red Deer, Alberta, Canada, when teachers found a bomb-threat note. They immediately went into action. Did they go into "lockdown"? Did they evacuate the school and call in the bomb squad? Nope. Some of the teachers actually sent students out to search lockers to try to find the bomb. There was even a competition among the students of one class, offering a prize to whoever found the bomb first.

The Morgan Community College in Fort Morgan, Colorado, was awarded an emergency grant of $75,000. The money was needed after it was discovered that because of **"an oversight in the plan"** for the just-finished **student center building,** the structure was built without rest rooms.

A University of Arkansas football coach commenting on a decision by a freshman to forfeit his football scholarship and return home: **"He signed with us just to get [an engineering] education, and that's the wrong reason. I wish he had told us that [sooner]."**

Tic-Tac-Don't

A nine-year-old student from Weems Elementary School in Manassas, Virginia, was suspended under the school's zero-tolerance policy on drugs. The boy had been caught giving his friend a Certs breath mint. The school policy not only bans real drugs but also "look-alikes" that a reasonable person would believe is a controlled substance. Defending his son's reputation, the boy's father said, "He's not a breath-mint addict or anything like that." Not yet, but who knows where something like this might lead?

A fourth-grade student from Panama City, Florida, was reading a magazine in class when **his teacher grabbed the magazine, ripped it up, and threw it in the trash can.** The teacher accused the young boy of bringing pornography to school, but it turned out the child was looking at the illustrations in a rare collector's issue of *National Geographic*.

Crack That Whip!

To compete with students' love for collectible cards (i.e., Baseball, Pokémon, etc.), the Ministry of Education in New Brunswick, Canada, published a set of their own "safety cards." The cards supplied students with tips on issues ranging from Internet safety to dealing with bullies. The ministry hoped the cards would become popular but they didn't expect the overwhelming response they received. The most coveted card was the one dealing with Internet safety that included a Web site address directing children to a site dealing in detail with the topic. But the URL directed children to a Web site called "Erotic female domination," which featured "women, scantily clad in leather, whipping and humiliating naked men." Officials requested that teachers and parents either return or destroy the cards. Who says education can't be fun?

Approximately twenty female students from a Salinas, California, high school held a protest upon hearing that the school's dress code banned thong underwear. **"We wear thongs!"** chanted the protesters. The demonstration finally broke up after the principal explained that the school's dress code does not, and never has, banned thong underwear.

Hey, Idiot!

Essay What?

An English teacher in Franklin, Ohio, got a little too creative in assigning essay questions to her students. She posed the question: "If you had to assassinate one famous person who is alive right now, who would it be and how would you do it?" If students didn't want to work on that essay question they could choose the alternative: "If you had to lose everyone you know in a tragic accident except one person," who would that person be and why? The school's principal refused to identify the teacher in front of outraged parents and explained that the essay topics were "inappropriate," but he would take no further action. I'll bet the parents could easily write five hundred words on that decision.

A former elementary school teacher in Wichita Falls, Texas, challenged the state's attempt to have his teaching certificate revoked. The man claimed his teaching ability was a **"gift from God,"** despite his admission that he had stolen a student's prescription of Ritalin, cooked it down, and shot up with it.

Hey, Idiot!

Sex Education

While diligently working on an exam, a group of students from a prestigious private school in Wiltshire, England, looked up from their set of questions to see a set of naked breasts. Apparently the teacher watching over the exam had logged onto a porno site on the Internet and was watching over naked pictures of women. The teacher must have had his eyes glued to the computer screen because he didn't notice his computer was hooked up to the large video monitor in the room. Commenting on this occurrence, the principal said, "Three weeks ago, while invigilating a practice examination for 17 pupils, [the teacher] used the computer and entered a website for 13 minutes containing still photographs of naked adult women." The principal concluded with "[The teacher] is currently on sick leave." If the students were studying the laws of probability I'll bet they could easily calculate the outcome of this situation.

The Western Illinois University men's basketball team had already played several games in their new jerseys before someone noticed that **"Illinois" was spelled "Illinios."** The team played all their games in their "away" jerseys for the rest of the season.

Stripped off the Team

A female student at California State Fullerton was forced by her track coach to either quit the team or quit her part-time job. The student eventually made the decision to quit the team and not give up her night job as an exotic dancer—which is how she could afford to go to college in the first place. Her coach said allowing her to strip after school "would detract from the image and accomplishments of her teammates, the athletic department and the university." So how did the coach find out about the girl's profession? Members of the school's baseball team attended the club where she performed and caught her act. Commenting on the coach's criticism of "the image and accomplishments of . . . the university," the stripper explained that while members of the baseball team in the audience were wearing school caps and sweaters, she doesn't wear any clothing that identifies her school in the act.

A female student at Penn State University complained to local authorities that **she was the victim of fraud.** The woman told police that she had given a fellow student a $1,200 stereo and in exchange the student agreed to take an exam for her. The complaint was submitted when the student failed the exam and then refused to return the stereo.

Hey, Idiot!

Even More Notes from Home

My daughter was absent yesterday because she was tired. She spent a weekend with the Marines.

Please excuse Jason for being absent yesterday. He had a cold and could not breed well.

Please excuse Mary for being absent yesterday. She was in bed with gramps.

Gloria was absent yesterday as she was having a gangover.

Please excuse Burma, she has been sick and under the doctor.

Maryann was absent December 11–16, because she had a fever, sore throat, headache and upset stomach. Her sister was also sick, fever and sore throat, her brother had a low grade fever and ached all over. I wasn't the best either, sore throat and fever. There must be something going around, her father even got hot last night.

A fourth-grade teacher from Rockaway Township, New Jersey, **couldn't believe his ears** when the principal accused him of coming to class intoxicated. The teacher drove himself to the police station and demanded a Breathalyzer. He failed and was arrested for DUI.

John Q. Idiot

Hey, Idiot!

I Think I Can. I Think I Can. I Think I Can.

CSX railroad police watched as a thirty-year-old Nashville, Tennessee, man placed a twenty-foot ladder across two different train tracks and waited for a train to come along. The police removed the ladder before a calamity could happen and promptly arrested the man. When asked why he had put the ladder across the tracks in the first place, the man explained that he had stolen the ladder and found it too cumbersome, so he put it on the tracks in hopes a train would come by and make two ten-foot ladders out of it. He was sentenced to six months in jail—or another way of looking at it is that he was sentenced to one-half of a one-year sentence.

An Elkhart, Indiana, man has been charged with armed bank robbery, using a firearm during the course of a violent crime, and felony firearms violations. The **charges don't seem out of the ordinary** until you realize the man was the founder of the city's gun buy-back program, Drop Your Guns.

You're an Animal

Actual calls received by the British RSPCA (Royal Society for the Prevention of Cruelty to Animals):

- A woman claiming that the "Beast of Bodmin Moor" was outside her door and laying siege to her house. The "beast" turned out to be her new telephone books in a black plastic bag.

- A person who reported a dead horse floating in a flooded area that turned out to be a plank of wood.

- A person who reported a black swan trapped on a building roof that ended up being a black plastic bag flapping in the wind.

- A person who called to report an injured magpie on his driveway, but it ended up being a black-and-white Nike sneaker.

A Turkish **truck driver was killed** when he tried to warm up the frozen diesel fuel by lighting a fire under his truck.

Hey, Idiot!

A Teenager and a Piece of Tail

While on a diving trip off the Florida Keys with his family, a sixteen-year-old Rockford, Illinois, youth became fascinated with a shark swimming nearby. So he did what any person who is underwater in the company of sharks would do—he pulled on the shark's tail. The shark, being a shark, did what any shark in the same situation would do—he chomped down on the boy's chest and wouldn't let go. The boy swam back to the diving vessel and was pulled aboard, shark still clinging on. The captain radioed the Coast Guard, which took the boy and the shark by boat and then ambulance to Fisherman's Hospital. A doctor had to split the three-foot nurse shark's spine in order to unlock its jaw. The teenager was released the same day—the shark didn't pull through.

A forty-three-year-old man from Richmond, Virginia, was hospitalized after being blown off the top of a van traveling fifty miles per hour. Authorities said the man had been lying on top of the van holding down a bundle of wooden fencing when **a gust of wind blew him off.**

Reach Out and Touch Someone

A Saegertown, Pennsylvania, man was tired of looking out his window and seeing two ugly telephone service boxes at the edge of his property. So he took matters into his own hands and, with the help of his trusty tractor, ripped out the ugly boxes. His little hands-on cleaning program not only made his property look better, it also knocked out telephone service to approximately 104 Alltel telephone customers. "Apparently the boxes were ripped from the ground," said Susan Poux, an Alltel area manager. The customers were reconnected the next morning. The accused man could not be reached for comment—his phone is no longer in service.

A sixteen-year-old boy was arrested in Sarasota, Florida, on charges of assaulting his mother because she and her boyfriend **refused to share their marijuana** with him.

A Blast from the Past

A woman simply trying to tidy up her house caused mayhem in her community—police closed off a section of her street and frightened parents took their children from the Jewish Community Center in her neighborhood. The Maitland, Florida, woman wanted to get rid of a "hunk of junk" that had been in her house since she moved there. She lugged the heavy metal object out of her house and placed it next to the other garbage for pickup day. A U.S. Army bomb squad was called out when the metal object turned out to be a World War II flash bomb. The woman had no idea what had been in her house for years. "My kids and I have picked it up millions of times," she said. Further investigation revealed the bomb had been defused and was not a threat. "I understand someone being scared, in retrospect," she said.

A British schoolboy was rushed to the hospital on a city bus when **he was unable to remove a vase that was stuck on his head.** According to eyewitnesses, in a vain effort to make the boy look more normal, his mother had placed his school cap on top of the vase.

Hey, Idiot!

A Marriage Shot to Hell

A California couple were scheduled to attend a marriage counseling session together, but the husband arrived late. The wife was so enraged that she pulled a pistol out of her pocket and shot her husband. He returned fire with a gun he had in his waistband. Both have been charged with attempted murder. The meeting was held at their local church.

A twenty-three-year-old man from Chandler, Arizona, called police because he had accidentally lost the keys to a set of handcuffs that he was currently wearing. **Police arrived at the scene** and ran a search on the man's name— there was a warrant out for his arrest, and police took him to jail in his own cuffs.

Hey, Idiot!

Tomb Raider

India's Baroda Museum reported that irreparable damage had been done to a priceless three-thousand-year-old Egyptian mummy. Curators reported that an overzealous cleaning woman had opened the glass case containing the mummy and had vacuumed the entire wrapped body, removing ancient dust and peeled toe paint, loosening all the bandages, and sucking off part of the nose. To make sure the dirty old mummy looked its best, the woman went so far as to scrub it down with soap and water.

A farmer in Lexington, Kentucky, claimed that a space alien **"walked with prissy little steps and swished his shoulders back and forth"** in an attempt to seduce him.

Animals à la Carte

More than eight hundred people were on hand to place bids in a most unusual auction held in Munich, Germany. Were they bidding on paints, furniture, or antiques? Nope. They were bidding on animals that had been killed in traffic accidents. Some bidding became fierce, with more than $1,300 going for a near perfect carcass of a stag. People on hand said they attended the auction to either mount the animals as trophies or stock their freezers with exotic, legal meat. Road Kill Restaurant: You kill it, we grill it.

An animal lover in Wisconsin found a hamster on his way to work one cold, rainy morning and took pity on the creature. He **cradled the shivering animal in his hands** and knew he had to find a warm place for the furry rodent so he gently placed it in his front pants pocket. The animal apparently didn't like his new habitat and tried to bite his way out, severely wounding the Good Samaritan's genitals.

Hey, Idiot!

Curl Up and Dye

An upset woman burst into the Clipping Company salon in Renton, Washington, demanding to use the telephone. Customers were startled by the woman, who claimed she had parked in a handicapped space, even though she isn't handicapped, and that a handicapped motorist had damaged her car in retaliation for her taking the spot. She yelled at the customers, "It's nobody's business where I park!" The woman wanted to use the phone to call police to report the other driver. Police arrived not to take her statement but to take her downtown—she was ticketed for parking in a handicapped spot without a permit.

A driving instructor from Parkersburg, West Virginia, was **allowed to keep his job** as a driving instructor at the local high school—even though he was arrested for drunk driving.

Send in the Clowns

A real estate investor thought he had struck it rich when he looked over an abandoned bank and happened upon a package of bills in an open vault. The thirty-year-old man from Richmond Hill, Georgia, stuffed the money in his pocket and slowly headed for the door—not realizing that it was a dummy pack that bank tellers give to robbers. The pack suddenly exploded, covering the man with red dye and an irritant much like tear gas. The red-faced real estate agent ran to the truck he had borrowed from a friend who worked as a clown, and quickly donned the clown suit in order not to stain the interior of the truck. Apparently, the dye irritated his skin to such a degree that the man jumped out of the truck and headed toward the First Bank of Coastal Georgia to get help. Employees of the bank, seeing a man in a clown suit covered with red dye and jumping up and down, alerted police to a potential robbery. After listening to the real estate agent's story, the chief of police decided not to file charges and stated, "Nothing this unusual has ever occurred that I can remember."

Every year in the United States, about eight thousand people are **seriously injured by toothpicks.**

Hey, Idiot!

Takes One to Know One

A couple in Englewood, Colorado, were out on their first date and having a great time together eating barbecue and drinking wine. The woman, an emergency room nurse, started telling stories of accidental gunshot wounds people had inflicted on themselves. The man, a former Air Force pilot, agreed with his date's opinion that the people who accidentally shot themselves were indeed stupid as they didn't know about simple gun safety rules. To prove his point he pulled out his 9 mm pistol—and accidentally shot himself in the leg.

Wanted: Somebody to go back in time with me. This is not a joke. You'll get paid after we get back. Must bring your own weapons. Safety not guaranteed. I have only done this once before.

—*Actual want ad from the* Oakview (California) Gazette

Suicide? Homicide? Insecticide?

A man from Ennetbaden, Switzerland, was seen plunging fifty-nine feet from his attic window, bouncing off the roof of his building onto the canopy of a restaurant, and finally crashing into the Limmat River. He was pulled from the river suffering only slight injuries. Was he pushed from the window? Was it a suicide attempt? Nope, the man had climbed on top of his radiator in an attempt to swat a fly when he lost his balance and plummeted out the window.

A man on a water scooter on Lake Michigan was missing for two days when Coast Guard personnel finally located him sitting on his scooter **suffering from sunstroke and dehydration.** The man hadn't had any water for two days, confusing the Coast Guard because Lake Michigan is a freshwater lake.

White-Line Fever

The following are real answers received on exams given by the California Department of Transportation's driving school:

Q: Do you yield when a blind pedestrian is crossing the road?
A: What for? He can't see my license plate.

Q: Who has the right of way when four cars approach a four-way stop at the same time?
A: The pickup truck with the gun rack and the bumper sticker saying, "Guns don't kill people. I do."

Q: When driving through fog, what should you use?
A: Your car.

Q: What changes would occur in your lifestyle if you could no longer drive lawfully?
A: I would be forced to drive unlawfully.

Q: What are some points to remember when passing or being passed?
A: Make eye contact and wave "hello" if he/she is cute.

Q: What is the difference between a flashing red traffic light and a flashing yellow traffic light?
A: The color.

Q: How do you deal with heavy traffic?
A: Heavy psychedelics.

Condom-Nation

After dinner, drinks, and dancing, a couple in Madrid, Spain, were planning on topping off the night by making love. The man pulled into a pharmacy on a popular beach in Cádiz in southern Spain and found a condom machine. He put coins in the machine, turned the knob, and nothing happened. He pounded on the machine, frantically turned the knob, and cursed loudly, but nothing happened. In desperation he stuck his hand into the dispenser slot to try to loosen the condoms. While wiggling his fingers inside the machine he quickly realized something was wrong—his fingers were stuck. Try as he might he couldn't get his hand out of the condom machine. For more than two hours the man's hand remained jammed in the machine while passersby made lurid comments. Finally the fire department arrived and removed the machine from the wall with the man's hand still attached and took him to the station to remove it. Needless to say, the mood was ruined, and there's no word on whether the man ever got his condom. But we do know what he didn't get.

A Jefferson Township, New Jersey, **woman obviously not watching what she was doing** grabbed a bottle of SuperGlue instead of her eyedrops and accidentally glued her eye shut.

Controlled Substance

A nineteen-year-old Albuquerque, New Mexico, man went on a tirade, beating up his girlfriend and threatening to kill members of her family. It was truly a night of terror for the woman's family who, seeing what he had done to his girlfriend, knew the man was capable of murder. The reign of terror ended finally after the man told his girlfriend he had put poison in her drink but that he had accidentally drunk it himself. The man lost consciousness after falling and hitting his head on a coffee table.

Police thought the driver of an armored truck in Edmonton, Alberta, **was trying to signal for help** by repeatedly opening and closing the truck's door. Calling for backup, the original officer and five other patrol cars pulled the armored car over to find out what the problem was. It turned out there wasn't an emergency; the driver was simply trying to fan fresh air into the cab after his partner had passed gas.

Balloon Animals

Two young men from Tampa, Florida, thought they had a great way of creating inexpensive fireworks for the Independence Day celebration. They filled up about ten balloons with acetylene gas. They were heading to a party, so they loaded up one of the men's car with the explosive balloons, got in, and slammed the door. A spark ignited the balloons, blowing up the car and projecting the two men several feet into the air. The car "looked like a sardine can," said a Tampa police bomb technician. "It was as if you just took the roof and peeled it off." Both men suffered burns, bruises, and hearing loss.

— — — — — — — — — —

A caller reported at 7 p.m. Sunday that a man was holding a knife to a woman in a car parked in the Albertson's parking lot. Officers responded and determined that the woman was actually using the man's knife to clean her teeth.

—*From the* Bozeman (Montana) Daily Chronicle

The Light's on but No One's Home

Four teenage boys from Gillingham, Kent, stashed away food and alcohol in a loft waiting for the perfect time to have a secret party. The opportunity arose when one of the boys' mothers went out of town. "We went up to get the food and drink from our loft after we had stashed it there because we didn't want our parents to find out," said one. The boys were beside themselves with joy knowing they would have the run of the house while the parent was gone for four days. They scurried up to the loft to get their hidden stash and closed the trapdoor behind them. With their hands full of goodies they pushed on the door to get out—it didn't budge. They kept pushing and pushing more and more frantically, trying to get out, until they realized they were stuck there. Trapped in a loft with nothing to eat except a lot of food and booze. After seventeen hours one of the boys decided to give the door another go and this time, instead of pushing the door, he tried pulling on the handle. The door opened right up. The expression "they had cobwebs in their attic" was true of these four lads.

A thirty-two-year-old man from Willard, Kentucky, accidentally shot himself in the thigh **while practicing his quick draw on a snowman.**

Stowaway We Go!

A thirty-six-year-old man from Nanaimo, British Columbia, tried to stow away on a ship as it left Vancouver—the hard way. The man positioned himself on a bridge, knowing the ship would pass under him. He had a bungee cord firmly tied around his waist, and he planned to jump down onto the ship's deck, cut the cord, and gain a free cruise. As soon as the ship was in position, the man leapt from the bridge but he hadn't properly calculated the weight of his body, the distance of the fall, and the tension of the cord. Instead of gracefully landing a few feet from the deck, the man slammed onto the ship's tennis court and then bounced back up. On his way back down he crashed into the railing of the stern and was left dangling above the water like a yo-yo. He rappelled into the water, where the crew of a passing boat rescued him. Life has its little ups and downs, but this guy had them all in one day.

An unnamed man in Modesto, California, was rushed to the hospital after **his skull was fractured by a brick.** Police investigating the accident soon realized there was no foul play and that the man had simply been tying to toss the brick as high in the air as he could. Since it was dark, he lost sight of the object until it landed on his head.

A Crappy Idea

A man entered the rest room at an international hamburger chain in Stockholm, Sweden, and was surprised to find all the toilet seats were missing. He went to the counter to inquire about their whereabouts, and he saw an employee pulling the newly washed toilet seats out of a dishwasher, where they had been washed alongside trays and serving utensils. The manager tried to comfort the disgusted man by assuring him that freshly washed toilet seats would be both warm and pleasant to sit on. Makes you wonder how they cleaned the urinals, doesn't it?

Police in Middlefield, Ohio, spotted a vehicle heading down a stretch of road with the driver fast asleep. The officer gave chase, trying to get the driver to wake up and regain control of the vehicle. The police officer didn't turn on his siren because **he didn't want to spook the horse.** You see, the driver was a seventeen-year-old Amish boy, and the vehicle was his horse-drawn carriage. Eventually, the buggy crashed into a police cruiser that tried to stop the horse by pulling in front of it. The horse was slightly injured but is expected to make a full recovery. The boy was charged with DUI.

I'll Take a Whack at It?

While taking a break from digging a foundation for an addition to his friend's home, an Englishman looked out to see his friend flailing on his back. "I'd gone inside to make a drink and looked out to see him kicking his leg violently. His other hand was on a pickax embedded in the soil. I thought he had hit a live wire." In order to save his friend's life, the man quickly grabbed a shovel and whacked the man in the chest in an attempt to knock him clear of the current. But the man hadn't hit an electric wire and was terrified to see his friend coming after him with a shovel—believing he had gone insane. So what was the problem? Apparently a wasp had flown up the trouser leg of the first man, and he was frantically kicking his leg trying to get the wasp to fly out when his friend attacked him with a shovel. Although the man missed work for three weeks because of a dislocated shoulder, he said, at least the wasp didn't sting him. And really, what are friends for?

A Hardwick, Georgia, woman divorced her husband on the grounds that he **"stayed home too much and was much too affectionate."**

Erotic Idiots

This Thing Sucks!!!!

In a classic case of "It seemed like a good idea at the time," a fifty-one-year-old Long Branch, New Jersey, man screamed "Eureka!" after he stuck his penis in his vacuum cleaner. The vacuum did more than clean those high-traffic areas—it also chopped off a half inch of the drunken man's penis. When officers first arrived on the scene, the man tried to convince them he had been stabbed in the crotch as he slept. But Long Branch public safety director Louis Napoletano soon realized the man was hoping for sexual gratification when he tried to put his own attachment in the vacuum. "What he didn't realize is that there's a blade in the vacuum cleaner right under where the hose attaches that pushes the dust into the collection bag," Napoletano said. And it was in the collection bag that authorities found the rest of the man's hose. Doctors at Monmouth Medical Center were able to bring the bleeding under control but were unable to reattach the severed part.

Remember, folks, "Drinking and vacuuming don't mix!"

Donald Duck comics were banned in Finland because **he doesn't wear pants.**

Don't Screw Around with Amtrak

Amtrak personnel evacuated most of the train station in Springfield, Massachusetts, after hearing a "ticking sound" inside a piece of luggage. After failing to contact the owner of the luggage, police opened the bag and found a vibrating sex toy. Soon the toy's owner showed up, claimed his luggage, claimed his toy, and clammed up. "I don't know who this guy was going to see in Atlanta. He must have been pretty red in the face," said Lieutenant Robert Thibodeau.

"[The victim] also has difficulty sleeping, driving his manual car, and has lost his libido," ruled an Australian judge, who also awarded $432,000 to a fifty-four-year-old man who lost his sex drive after being attacked by a pig.

Stupid Sex Laws—Part 1

In Connorsville, Wisconsin, it's illegal for a man to shoot off a gun when his female partner has an orgasm.

It's against the law in Willowdale, Oregon, for a husband to curse during sex.

In Oblong, Illinois, it's punishable by law to make love while hunting or fishing on your wedding day.

No man is allowed to make love to his wife with the smell of garlic, onions, or sardines on his breath in Alexandria, Minnesota. If his wife so requests, law mandates that he must brush his teeth.

Bozeman, Montana, has a law that bans all sexual activity between members of the opposite sex in the front yard of a home after sundown—if they're nude.

Lost in the Translation

A sign posted in Germany's Black Forest:

IT IS STRICTLY FORBIDDEN ON OUR BLACK FOREST CAMPING SITE THAT PEOPLE OF DIFFERENT SEX, FOR INSTANCE, MEN AND WOMEN, LIVE TOGETHER IN ONE TENT UNLESS THEY ARE MARRIED WITH EACH OTHER FOR THAT PURPOSE.

Put a Plug in It

Annoyed neighbors took a German couple to court because they made too much noise while having sex. A court ordered the verbal violators to tone down the volume during their lovemaking sessions or face stiff penalties (I had to say it). Any future violations of the court order may result in a substantial fine and/or two years in prison.

Four on the Floor

Two "love birds" from Naples, Italy, were fooling around in their subcompact car at a local lovers' lane ("You put your foot in the glove box and I'll rest my elbow in the cup holder . . .") when they were accidentally hit from behind. The couple claimed they "lost control" during the collision and are suing to recover the expenses of their unplanned pregnancy. I guess the airbags weren't the only things that deployed.

Two in the Bush

A Peeping Tom in Melbourne, Australia, was caught spying on what he thought was a beautiful naked woman. He was found crouching behind some bushes and arrested for lewd behavior. What was he eyeballing? A full-figured, undressed mannequin. I guess he could brag to his friends that he was spying on a model.

Leave the Driving to Us

A few years ago if you needed information about the bus schedule in Madison County, Illinois, you might call the Transit District phone number. A very friendly operator would get on the line and say, "You need it bad, and we've got it good," but she wasn't talking about buses. A mix-up occurred when the phone company accidentally listed a 1-900 phone-sex number instead of the number for the Madison County Transit District. No one is sure how the mix-up came about, and the problem has been corrected. Warning: In case of emergency—pull cord.

STATE: SEX WITH MINOR WORTH FELONY CHARGE
—El Paso Times

Hey, Idiot!

Reach Out and Touch Yourself

After a long night of drinking a man from Troy, New York, went home alone and decided to try his luck on the phone. He wasn't calling up an old girlfriend—he called a 1-900 European phone sex line charging $9.95 per minute. Several hours later he finally finished his call and hung up, tallying an impressive $7,164 bill. Was this man simply insatiable? Nope, he fell asleep after making the call and the line stayed connected. I wonder if he was just trying to call the bus company.

The European Commission has issued **new public health guidelines** and translated them into nine languages. They recommend that prostitutes involved in sadomasochism be educated on how to sterilize their whips.

Hey, Idiot!

Let's Make a Deal

The following excerpt was taken from a criminal report from the Charleston, West Virginia, Police Department:

27 July 99 approx. 0211 hrs. Detective E. D. Randle and I were working a plainclothes assignment on the West Side when the defendant drove up. Det. Randle was writing citations to 3 suspected prostitutes. The defendant apparently thought that Det. Randle and I were "pimping" the females out. With my police badge around my neck under a streetlight, the defendant stated that he wanted one of the girls and that he had $20. The defendant stated other specifics as to what he wanted, at which point I told him he was under arrest.

Sigurder Hjartarson of Reykjavik, Iceland, has meticulously collected eighty-two specimens from thirty-six different species of animals and has opened **the world's first penis museum.**

Keep on Truckin'

A Peruvian couple thought they had found the perfect spot for a session of hot lovemaking—a tractor-trailer truck. Did they sneak into the cab and mess around or did they crawl into the empty trailer for their tryst? Nope, for some reason they crawled under the truck and, yes, you guessed it, were seriously injured when the driver of the truck showed up and drove away. For a second there, I'm sure they didn't know if they were coming or going.

TEENAGE GIRLS OFTEN HAVE BABIES FATHERED BY MEN
—Sunday Oregonian

Stupid Sex Laws—Part 2

An ordinance in Newcastle, Wyoming, specifically bans couples from having sex while standing inside a store's walk-in meat freezer!

It is illegal to make love on the floor between beds in motels in North Carolina.

In Kentucky, "No female shall appear in a bathing suit on any highway within this state unless she be escorted by at least two officers or unless she be armed with a club." But "The provisions of this statute shall not apply to females weighing less than 90 pounds nor exceeding 200 pounds nor shall it apply to female horses."

It is illegal to make love in your car in Detroit, Michigan, unless it is parked on your own property.

Eureka, Nevada, law: "A mustache is a known carrier of germs and a man cannot wear one if he habitually kisses human beings."

Sealed with a Kiss

A Prestonsburg, Kentucky, man has filed a lawsuit against a forty-nine-year-old woman, demanding $1,500 or fifteen sessions of sex. The man claims that he had an agreement with the woman for a "sex for money deal." His lawsuit states that he agreed to pay the woman $100 per sex session and that he had fronted her $1,800 against eighteen sexual acts. The man claims they had only three sexual encounters and is now demanding a return of his remaining $1,500 or fulfillment of the original agreement. Taking someone to court over sex and money will result in only one outcome—you'll get screwed and the lawyers will get all the money.

Sex workers in New Zealand **can claim the cost of bubble bath,** dairy whip, condoms, lubricants, gels, oils, tissues, lingerie, costumes, and see-through garments against their income tax. It must be great to be a CPA in New Zealand.

Hey, Idiot!

The Key to Happiness

Two lovers in the United Kingdom decided to spice up their sex life with the help of a pair of handcuffs. Everything was going great until they discovered something was missing—the key. Try as they might, they were unable to free themselves and eventually had to call local police to come and give them a hand.

In addition to serving prison time, the Johor Baru Religious Affairs Department in Malaysia recently announced that convicted sexual **"deviants"** would be bound and whipped.

Hey, Idiot!

Next Time Try the Bus

A Swedish taxi driver was convicted of overcharging a forty-nine-year-old woman after he left the meter running while he had sex with her. According to the *Aftonbladet* newspaper, the driver billed the woman $8,300 for "sexual services." The itemized bill included 25 percent sales tax, plus charges for trips, hotel, and telephone calls. What, a 15 percent gratuity wasn't automatically tallied in?

A Michigan jury awarded $200,000 to a twenty-seven-year-old man who claimed a car accident transformed him into a homosexual. For irony's sake, **I hope it was a rear-end collision.**

Hey, Idiot!

Once, Twice, Three Times a Lady

A twenty-four-year-old woman in Beloit, Wisconsin, was charged with battery for allegedly hitting her husband with a plant stand, sending him to the hospital for six stitches. According to the police statement, the newlyweds frequently fought about sex. The night of the attack the woman became enraged because her husband decided to call it quits after only four sexual encounters with her that day.

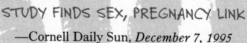

STUDY FINDS SEX, PREGNANCY LINK
—Cornell Daily Sun, *December 7, 1995*

Stupid Sex Laws—Part 3

Ashland, Kentucky: "No person shall knowingly keep or harbor at his house or her house within the city any women of ill-repute, lewd character, or a common prostitute—other than wife, mother, or sister."

It is illegal to hang male and female underwear on the same line in Minnesota.

It is illegal to wink at any female person with whom you are unacquainted in Ottumwah, Iowa.

Seattle, Washington: No female is allowed to ride on a bus or train while sitting upon a man's lap—unless, that is, a pillow is first placed between them. The possible jail sentence for a female who violates this law? An automatic six months (the man involved isn't prosecuted.)

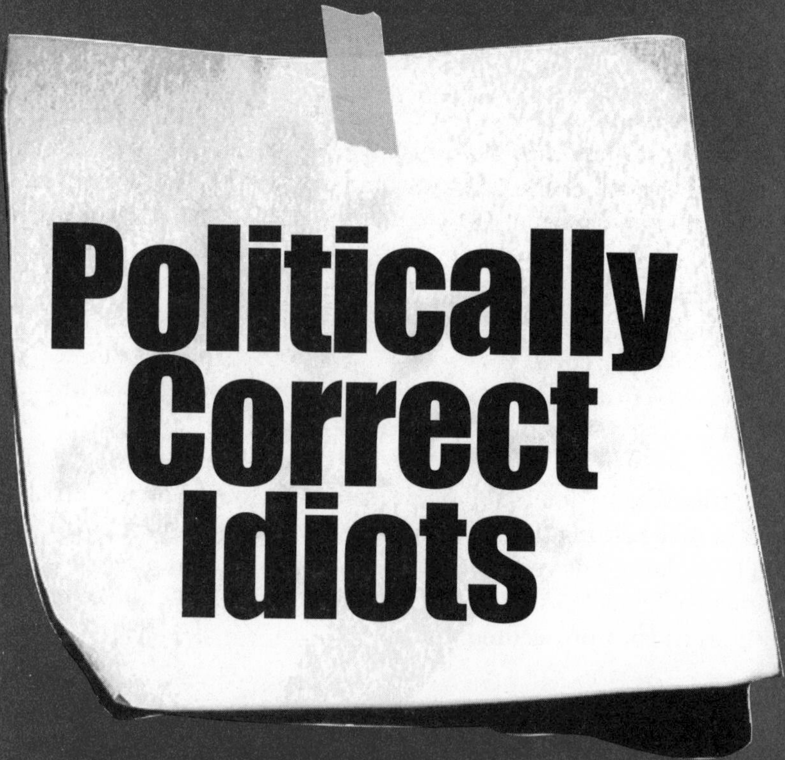
Politically
Correct
Idiots

Hey, Idiot!

Waiting to Exhale

A thirteen-year-old girl who suffers from acute asthma began having an asthma attack on the school bus ride home. She didn't have her inhaler with her, and her breathing was becoming more and more labored. A quick-thinking friend who also has asthma reached into her bag, pulled out her own inhaler, and gave it to her classmate. Both of the girls' mothers considered the act to be heroic and worthy of an award. But school officials, citing their zero-tolerance policy against drugs, have labeled the girl who handed over her inhaler a "drug trafficker." It is a notation that will stay on her school record for three years. Zero tolerance for the heroic schoolgirl. Zero intelligence for the school board. I don't know about you, but that decision leaves me breathless.

The Walworth County, Wisconsin, City Council, in drafting an antibigotry resolution, changed a reference to white supremacist organizations from **"hate groups" to "unhappy groups."**

Hey, Idiot!

Addled Ads

The *Seattle Times* placed an article in its real estate section explaining that it is obligated, under the Fair Housing Act, to warn potential advertisers to refrain from using words or phrases that hint of tenant preference. The red-flag words are: "Adult, Bachelor, Couple, Family (as in 'perfect for family'), Mature, No Children, One Person, Retired ('housing for the elderly' is considered), Sex (may be acceptable in advertising for roommates), Single, Two People, Christian, Executive, Handicap (as in 'not suitable for'—but okay for 'handicap accessible'), Integrated, Membership Approval, Mentally Ill, Religious, Religious Landmark (near St. Peter's, the Synagogue, the Mosque, etc.), Older Persons or Senior Citizens (housing communities designed for elderly may be acceptable), Physically Fit Person, Private ('private community' is a big no-no; 'private drive' is fine), Race, Restricted, Senior Discount." So, basically, ads for homes should read: "For sale—house."

A committee formed to create a diversity education program for incoming freshmen at the University of Pennsylvania listed as an example of sexual discrimination not allowed on campus **"woman's name not remembered."**

Solo Act

One member of the University Planning Committee voiced concern when the University of Pennsylvania announced mandatory "racism seminars" for all their students. She said she felt mandatory seminars were unconstitutional and said she had "deep regard for the individual and my desire to protect the freedoms of all members of society." A university administrator sent the note back to the committee member with the word "individual" circled and in the margin had written, "This is a RED FLAG phrase today, which is considered by many to be RACIST. Arguments that champion the individual over the group ultimately privileges [sic] the individuals who belong to the largest or dominant group." Using this rationale, one can no longer say "She's a real individual." Instead "She's a real part of the group" is politically correct.

Residents of Longmont, Colorado, voted to abolish all **"Dead End"** signs and have replaced them with signs reading **"No Outlet."** The residents considered the **"Dead End"** signs as being too unpleasant. I wonder if they'll replace the **"Slow Children"** sign with **"Speed-Sensitive Offspring."**

Hey, Idiot!

A Picture Is Worth a Thousand Words

Because a publishing company was striving for diversity for diversity's sake, a freelance artist who illustrates children's readers received ten pages of single-spaced instructions setting forth "multicultural" guidelines. Here is a description of one of the pictures based on the instructions—the hero is a Hispanic boy. The picture also includes a set of African-American twins (one girl, one boy), an overweight Asian boy, a Native American girl, and a Caucasian girl born with a congenital malformation that gave her only three fingers on one hand. In order to eliminate stereotypes, the Hispanic boy's parents had to be white-collar workers and eat non-Hispanic food—"spaghetti and meatballs and a salad." The editor even made sure the salad was not stereotypical (although mixed greens should have taken care of that) by stating, "Make sure it's not iceberg: it should be something nice like endive." And just to round things out, the artist was instructed to draw, in the background, a senior citizen—jogging. What, no illustration of a cat and dog holding paws?

Boston Latin High School now refers to Chinese New Year's Day as **"Asian New Year's,"** regardless of the fact that other Asian cultures celebrate the New Year on different days.

You Can Say That Again

The North York Women Teachers' Association of Ontario, Canada, published a pamphlet for teachers called *Nonviolent Language,* which contained a list of "violent" or "militaristic" phrases and suggested alternatives. The brochure directs teachers to replace common expressions that might "arouse violent images" with "'catchy' nonviolent alternatives." Here are some examples from *Nonviolent Language.*

Violent Phrase	Alternative
Kill two birds with one stone	Get two for the price of one
There's more than one way to skin a cat	There are different ways to solve a problem
Take a stab at it	Go for it!
Get away with murder	Avoid consequences
It's an uphill battle	It's next to impossible
You're dead meat	You're in serious trouble
Kick it around	Consider the options
That's a low blow	That's outside the rules
Hit them where it hurts	Find their vulnerability
Crash the party	Show up anyway
Shoot yourself in the foot	Undermine your own position
Hit the computer key	Press the computer key
Blown out of the water	Reduced to nothing

I need this like I need a hole in the head. Or, said in the "catchy" alternative way, "I need this about as much as I don't need this."

Hey, Idiot!

It's in the Mix

The Dade County School Board regretfully informed a computer-consulting firm that it was ineligible as a vendor because the business was not minority-owned. A business can qualify as minority-owned only if one minority group controls 51 percent of its assets. The company in question, Data Industries, is owned as a fifty-fifty partnership between Charles Duval, a black man, and Paul Raifaizen, a Hispanic. A spokesman for the school board said he sympathized with Data Industries, but insisted that "a rule is a rule, and our rule says that there must be 51 percent ownership by one principal minority group." He went on to justify their decision by saying, "We're just trying to preserve the integrity of the system," explaining that the county wants a "clear-cut" owner to avoid having minority businesses "sell out to white males."

An essay by a junior high school student, **"What Christmas Means to Me and Why,"** was selected for publication in the school newspaper. The principal, citing separation of church and state, refused to run it unless the sentence **"It is also the day that Christians celebrate Christ's birth"** was changed to **"[Christmas] is also a day that people celebrate love."**

Who's the Real Dope?

Anti-drug groups petitioned an advertising agency in Canoga Park, California, to remove ads from 106 bus-stop benches on the grounds that the advertised product portrayed drugs in a favorable light. The product, Alterna Hemp Shampoo, is perfectly legal, but the agency pulled the ads after receiving numerous complaints because the word "hemp" was used. I wonder if the anti-drug group will turn their attention to the most positive depiction of drugs—the cooking pot!

One of the cases created by the moot court of the New York University Law School was based on the legal ramifications of custody rights of a lesbian mother. The court was forced to withdraw the pretend court case after receiving protests that **"writing arguments [against the mother's side] is hurtful to a group of people and thus harmful to all of us."**

Oh, Mammy

As part of a student festival at Indiana University, the Kappa Kappa Gamma sorority teamed up with the Sigma Alpha Mu fraternity to present a play set in a Laundromat where the laundry comes to life. In order to create the illusion that the clothes were alive, the students used an old theatrical trick; they wore black pants and black long-sleeve turtleneck sweaters and used black makeup on their faces and hands so they wouldn't be seen controlling the strings on the laundry. A group of black students on campus protested the performance, claiming that the Greeks were sponsoring a "minstrel show," and got them to apologize for performing in "blackface."

In response to the American Kennel Club's warning that certain breeds of dog were "not good" for children, the founder of the Dachshund Club of America (I kid you not) said: **"To say that all these dogs are 'this' and these dogs are 'that,' that's racism, canine racism."** Hey, that sounds like Kennel-Rationing to me.

Hey, Idiot!

Culture Quiz

In response to fierce protests from parents, New York City finally ended its automatic testing of children with Hispanic names for placement in bilingual-education classes. Under the now defunct policy, children of Hispanic origin who scored below the fortieth percentile on a standardized English exam (40 percent of all the students taking the test) were automatically placed in Spanish-language programs, even if they did not speak Spanish. *Qué???*

In a **"Green Earth"** policy, the Harvard Divinity School placed recycling bins around the campus to collect paper. The bins were originally labeled **"white"** and **"colored."** An anonymous prankster relabeled the **"colored"** bin to read **"paper of color."** To which school officials relabeled both bins, as **"bleached paper"** and **"dyed paper."**

Hey, Idiot!

A Buzz of Activity

According to the *Los Angeles Times,* the military drew criticism for its unusual military research on whether honeybees could be trained to detect land mines. The group Animal Protection Institute reprimanded the military and stated that insects "shouldn't be forced into military service" because they "aren't U.S. citizens." If it ever did happen, the next in line to join up would be Winnie the Pooh. Or, as he would be called, Private First Class Pooh!

Citing the school's **"zero-tolerance sexual harassment policy,"** administrators at the McElwain Elementary School in Thornton, Colorado, threatened to suspend a ten-year-old girl for repeatedly asking one boy if he liked her and her friends.

Hey, Idiot!

Just Another Day

The Hillsborough School Board in New Jersey jumped on the politically correct bandwagon by voting to ban the word "Halloween," since it is derived from All Hollow's Eve, denoting the day before the Christian Feast of All Saints' Day. Instead, the board came up with their own catchy alternative name: "Fall Festival Celebration." But not wanting to stop there, they put their stamp on "St. Valentine's Day," which is now referred to as "Special Person Day." I bet those "Special Person Day" cards are great, too. "Happy Special Person Day. You, regardless of your race, creed, sexual orientation, or natural origin, are special to me in a nonsexual, nonracist, completely nonaggressive, nonassertive manner, which you may or may not reciprocate to me."

An article in the *Fresno Bee* concerning the Massachusetts budget crisis had obviously been run through the **"politically correct spell checker,"** as it referred to new taxes that could put the state **"back in the African-American."**

Color Me Gone

Crayola changed the name of its "Indian Red" crayon to distance itself from politically correct activists. The name of the color dates back centuries and is based on a reddish-brown pigment found near the country of India. However, Crayola decided to change the name anyway because it had received numerous letters from teachers who say students think the color is a derogatory reference to Native Americans. The new name for the color is "Chestnut." What? "Chest" and "nut" are sexist words if I've ever heard them!

An eight-year-old boy from South Elementary School in Jonesboro, Arkansas, was suspended under the school's "zero-tolerance" weapons policy. Did he have a knife or a gun? Nope, he was armed with a breaded chicken finger. The boy allegedly pointed the fried food at a teacher and said, "Pow, pow, pow" to her. The principal of the school defended the child's suspension, stating, **"People saw real threats to the safety and security of their students."**

Hey, Idiot!

It's Generic-Man

A group of students at the University of Massachusetts protested the use of the "Minuteman" as the school mascot. The organizer of the protests said the mascot is racist, sexist, and offensive to Native Americans since it portrays "a white man with a gun." The former mascot for the university, "Red Man," was discarded in 1972 because it was considered to be offensive to the Native American community.

New York Transit Authority officials admitted to hiring convicted criminals, but preferred to refer to them in the more PC terminology of **"criminally challenged," "legally impaired,"** or **"people of alternative conviction status."**

The National Aeronautics and Space Administration has stopped referring to its missions as **"manned"** and **"unmanned."** NASA now refers to missions as being **"habited"** and **"unhabited,"** or **"crewed"** and **"uncrewed."**

Hey, Idiot!

What's That Ringing Sound?

The Food and Drug Administration's *Equal Employment Opportunity Handbook* states: "The common requirement for 'knowledge of the rules of grammar' and 'ability to spell accurately' in secretarial job descriptions" should be eliminated because it may hinder the hiring of "underrepresented groups." Also, job interviews that "judge highly subjective traits such as motivation, ambition, maturity, personality, and neatness" should be eliminated. That'z the cind of jub I'm luking 4.

The Avery Coonley School in Illinois was banned for two years from the state science fair. **Had the school been caught cheating,** or were students engaging in illegal activities? Nope, they were barred from the fair because they had won the championship four years in a row, and officials wanted to give other schools a chance to win the title for a change.

Think Mink

The Animal Liberation Front, an animal rights extremist group, was condemned by animal lovers after they liberated six thousand minks from a fur farm in southern England. The minks, fairly ferocious weasel-type animals, were responsible for having "slaughtered" numerous house pets and farm animals. In order to defend their animals, authorities authorized people to kill any minks they encountered. "They are damned vicious, and I had to bash them," said a housewife who gained notoriety after killing several of the furry beasts with a shovel. Animal lovers also expressed dismay with the fact that, since the minks were raised in captivity, they didn't know how to forage for food, defend themselves from other animals, or protect themselves from the elements—many having frozen to death. Wow, if a mink froze to death, I guess those coats aren't very warm after all.

The Harrison County School Board in Mississippi banned a Jewish student from wearing a **Star of David** because it was feared that it might be mistaken for a gang symbol.

A Sour Outcome

The fire department and an ambulance were called to the Taylor Elementary School in Colorado Springs, Colorado, after a teacher saw a six-year-old boy give "drugs" to a fellow classmate. The parents of both boys were urged to take their children to the hospital for tests but the mother of the "dealer" refused. Why? Because, as the boy had tried to explain to school officials, he had given his friend a lemon drop bought in a health food store. An administrator at the school suspended the boy for half a day under the school's drug policy, which treats unfamiliar products as controlled substances. The mother called the response "complete hysteria," adding, "I can't believe these people are educating our kids." No telling what would have happened if the kid had given his friend a Twinkie.

The Sacramento Public Works Department sponsored a contest to find a new word to replace the definitely suggestive and possibly sexually offensive word **"manhole."** The response was tremendous and included such entries as **"sewer-viewer"** and **"person-access chamber."** The department didn't name a winner, but **"out of heightened awareness,"** they now refer to them as **"maintenance holes."**

Word Up

With summer approaching, a group of students at the Albany campus of the State University of New York decided to throw a "theme picnic" and chose to honor Baseball Hall of Famer Jackie Robinson, who broke baseball's color barrier. A gathering of about forty students protested the use of the word "picnic" to promote the event, insisting the word originally was a racist code word that referred to lynching blacks. The fact that any English teacher could have told them that "picnic" came into the English language in about 1750 and was derived from the French word *pique-nique,* which meant the same thing, wouldn't have deterred these naysayers. In fact, the school's affirmative action director released a memo asking everyone to stop using the word—regardless of its origin. "Whether the claims are true or not, the point is the word offended." The group throwing the, uh, event where you eat food outside on a blanket-type thing, changed the phrase to an "outing." But that word didn't sit too well with the campus's gay and lesbian community, and it was removed. So, after everyone had his or her say, the event was promoted without the use of a noun to describe what it was. Yogi Bear, the ultimate racist!

The San Francisco school district now officially refers to sex as **"penile-insertive behavior."**

Hey, Idiot!

Crash Course

A sociology professor at Ohio's Bowling Green State University noticed the political correctness craze and thought it would be an interesting topic on which to base a new course. He presented his "political correctness" course to his departmental colleagues, who turned down the proposal flat, as did other departments. Speaking on behalf of the Women's Studies department, which also rejected the course curriculum, one professor declared: "We forbid any course that says we restrict free speech."

A concerned parent noticed several basic errors, including an incorrect explanation for gravity, in his daughter's high school science textbook. He informed the publisher and hoped it would correct the errors in the next printing. The publishers wrote the father back and explained that they were aware of the errors, but that they were necessary evils in order to simplify the mathematics for **"enriched, average, and remedial students alike."**

The Play's the Thing

Students at King High School in Tampa, Florida, concerned about the rash of school shootings, staged a play sponsored by Mothers Against Violence in America to explore this frightening topic. The play, *Bang, Bang, You're Dead,* does not include a gun nor does it dramatize a shooting but simply depicts the victims of a fictional school shooting coming back to confront the student gunman on his motives and psychology, "making him realize how he's done something really, really horrible," according to King's drama teacher. The principal of the school said, "The moral of the story is a good one," but he banned students from attending the performance because its theme is of a "sensitive subject." And we wonder why our children have to go through metal detectors on their way to class.

In order to comply with the Americans with Disabilities Act, the Architectural and Transportation Barriers Compliance Board, an independent federal agency whose members are appointed by the president, ruled that all bank automated teller machines (ATMs), which cost banks nearly $10 billion to manufacture, **must be made accessible to the visually impaired.** The order included drive-up ATMs.

Athletic Idiots

Hey, Idiot!

Two's Company...

April 17, 1993—the Baltimore Orioles versus the California Angels. It was a play that had all the makings of a grand slam. The bases were loaded, and the Orioles only had one man out. Mike Devereaux stepped up to the plate and cracked the ball as hard as he could. The second the leather hit the wood, the runner at third, Jeff Tackett, headed for home. But Devereaux's line drive didn't make it to the wall and was caught by the Angels center fielder. Tackett shook his head and trotted back to third base. But when he got there he noticed his teammate, Brady Anderson, the runner from second, was standing on third. Standing next to Anderson was Chito Martinez—the runner from first. Angels catcher John Orton tagged all three—two were called out for an inning-ending double play. _Sports Illustrated_ called the play the stupidest play of the year. "It wouldn't have been the stupidest play until Chito arrived at third," said the California third baseman. "I think he thought there was a fight, so he ran across the field to get in it." Remember, folks: the players that hang out together get called out together.

During the 1991 World Series, **in the tenth inning of the seventh game,** Atlanta Braves owner Ted Turner fell asleep.

Not a Stock Ending

Stock car driver Danny Elko of Sydney, Australia, was speeding along at 205 miles an hour when he was involved in a five-car pileup. Amazingly, he survived with only a broken leg. He was placed in an ambulance and was heading to the hospital when the ambulance, traveling only 20 miles an hour, struck a guardrail. In a bizarre turn of events, the rear doors of the emergency response vehicle opened, tossing the wounded Elko out onto the pavement, where he fractured his skull and died.

This could ruin my career.

—*Darryl Strawberry to police officers after being arrested for solicitation and possession*

No Stomach for the Game

Both teams were in their stance. The ball was ready to be snapped. The quarterback was calling out the signals. Denver Bronco defensive tackle Darren Drozdov was in his position opposite the offensive center. It was the tense few milliseconds before the ball went into play during this August 1993 game when suddenly Drozdov made a messy defensive foul—he vomited on the ball. After the game Drozdov told reporters, "I get sick a lot. I was a quarterback in high school, and I'd start throwing up on my center's back. I don't have a lot of control out there." Well, at least his heart is in the right place.

— — — — — — — — — —

```
Winfield goes back to the wall.
He hits his head on the wall and
it rolls off! It's rolling all the
way back to second base! This is a
   terrible thing for the Padres!
```

—Jerry Coleman, Padres broadcast announcer

Marching to a Different Drummer

They'll never be called wimps and geeks again. During half-time at the Southern University versus Prairie View A&M game in Beaumont, Texas (September 1998), the teams' marching bands got into an on-field brawl that lasted twenty minutes. No one is sure of the particulars, but it started when the two marching bands passed each other in formation. When it was all over two $5,000 tubas were bent, and several pieces of uniform and one saxophone were listed as missing. It was a musical interlude that will live in the hearts and mind of both teams for quite some time. Talk about your battle of the bands.

If England are going to win this match, they're going to have to score a goal.

—*BBC commentator Jimmy Hill*

Hey, Idiot!

A Fishy Trade

Some baseball pitchers are worth their weight in gold—others, I guess, are only worth their weight in catfish. In one of the most bizarre trades in Western Baseball League history, the Oxnard, California, Pacific Suns swapped minor league pitcher Ken Krahenbuhl to the Greenville, Mississippi, Bluesmen for among other things—ten pounds of catfish. "I still can't believe they traded me for some catfish," Krahenbuhl said. "It's totally ridiculous." But the July 1998 trade turned out to be a good catch for the Bluesmen when Krahenbuhl pitched a perfect game for his new team. "The Suns could have gotten some players in exchange for me to help their ball club, instead of the stinking catfish, but they just don't care," he said. "They traded me for catfish. Can you believe that?" It's considered *one* of baseball's strangest trades but not the strangest. In 1997, the Greenville Bluesmen traded an unopened Muddy Waters record and fifty pounds of pheasant to Sioux Falls of the Northern League in exchange for a second baseman.

Fifty-eight-year-old Junuske Inoue, a Japanese billiards player, was suspended from competing for two years after he **tested positive for a muscle-building hormone.**

Hey, Idiot!

A Stroke of Bad Luck

During the final round of the 1934 U.S. Open, Bobby Cruickshank was ahead of his competitors by two strokes. In order to maintain his lead, he knew he had to make the next hole in four strokes. Cruickshank's drive from the tee was quietly applauded, and the ball rolled a respectable length down the fairway. Unfortunately, his follow-up shot was a clinker, and Cruickshank's hopes sank as he watched his ball sail into the stream in front of the green and disappear out of sight. But before his heart could skip a beat, Cruickshank and the amazed crowd watched as the ball bounced out of the stream (probably ricocheting off a submerged rock) and onto the green—an unbelievable ten feet from the hole. Cruickshank threw his club into the air, tipped the brim of his hat, and let out a yelp of gratitude to the heavens: "Thank you, God!" With his head so piously exposed and his attention focused on the ball and not the club—which at this time was hurtling toward the earth at a rapid rate—he smiled at the crowd. The club changed his expression when it clanked Cruickshank over the head, knocking him to the ground. He wasn't badly hurt by the falling five-iron, but he was unable to regain his composure or his sure-sightedness—he wound up third in the competition. Cruickshank was definitely teed off, but at least the falling club didn't give him a stroke.

Hey, Idiot!

Two Balls, No Strikes

Baseballs, caps, pennants, and other goodies are all part of promotional giveaways at baseball parks across the United States. Sometimes it's the giveaways that pull in the big crowds—not the team. Who can forget the mass appeal of those Beanie Babies? But the Charleston, South Carolina, River Dogs free promotion was as warmly received as, well, a free vasectomy—which is exactly what they offered. The minor-league River Dogs withdrew their Father's Day promotion of a free vasectomy the following day after fans protested. The clip job was nixed by the Roman Catholic Diocese of Charleston, spearheaded by Bishop David Thompson—a season ticket holder, mind you, and a father of a different sort. "We found that clearly people didn't like the idea," General Manager Mark Schuster said, adding that the promotion wasn't intended to offend anyone. "We are sensitive to our fans' wants." Makes that Beanie Babies craze seem a little more reasonable, doesn't it?

Upon hearing Joe Jacobi of the Washington Redskins say, **"I'd run over my own mother to win the Super Bowl,"** Matt Millen of the Raiders said, **"To win, I'd run over Joe's mom, too."**

Hey, Idiot!

The Sweet Spot

A high school baseball pitcher in Chicago filed a lawsuit against the makers of Louisville Slugger baseball bats. He claimed the company's aluminum bats are "unreasonably dangerous" to pitchers because they are designed to hit baseballs extremely hard.

— — — — — — — — — —

All I said was that the trades were stupid and dumb, and they took that and blew it all out of proportion.

—Minnesota Twins pitcher Ron Davis, defending a comment he made that criticized team managers for trading players

Hey, Idiot!

Out Like a Flash

The skies grew dark during a soccer match in the Democratic Republic of the Congo, but the fans kept watching, and the players kept playing. Nothing could dampen the game, they thought, not even a little rain. But then everyone at the game got the shock of their life when lightning crashed down, immediately killing all eleven members of the "away" team. Thirty other people received burns during the weekend match, and "The athletes from [the home team] Basanga curiously came out of this catastrophe unscathed," reported the Congo Press Agency.

I want all the kids to do what I do, to look up to me. I want all the kids to copulate me.

—*Chicago Cubs outfielder Andre Dawson on being a role model*

Hey, Idiot!

Deaf as a Post but Smart as a Fox

The Norfolk Blues were a team of collegiate all-stars and were considered by many, including themselves, to be the final word in college football. So when they were up against Gallaudet, they thought they had a sure thing—Gallaudet was the school for the hearing-impaired. Norfolk's egos were bigger than their helmets, and they decided that since their opponents were deaf, they wouldn't even bother calling out signals or going into huddles. This classic 1912 blunder ended in a shutout, 20 to 0, and the winners weren't the Norfolk Blues but the hearing-impaired Gallaudet. Why? Although Gallaudet's team was deaf they could still read lips and understood every play Norfolk was going to make. I'm sure that after the game, Norfolk's fans gave their team a few signs anyone could understand.

Julian Dicks is everywhere. It's like they've got eleven Dicks on the field.

—*Metro Radio sports commentary*

Hey, Idiot!

Boxer's Boxers

Featherweight boxer Richard Procter thought he was the local favorite after he jumped in the ring at the World Sporting Club in London. He tossed off his robe and listened to the thunderous applause from the crowd. It was only then that he realized he had forgotten to put his shorts on.

Two men **filed a lawsuit** against the stadium's concession stand at a Philadelphia Phillies baseball game, claiming the workers failed to fill the men's cups of beer to the rim.

Basketball great Charles Barkley of the Phoenix Suns **claimed that he was misquoted** in a book about his life and career. The book was his autobiography.

Hey, Idiot!

Nothing to Love

If you thought John McEnroe was the bad-mouthed bad boy of tennis—you ain't heard nothing yet. After fellow Zambian tennis player Musumba Bwayla beat Lighton Ndefwayl, he had this to say: "Musumba Bwayla is a stupid man and a hopeless player. He has a huge nose and is cross-eyed. Girls hate him. He beat me because my jockstrap was too tight, and because when he serves he farts, and that made me lose my concentration, for which I am famous throughout Zambia." Don't you just love a good sport?

- - - - - - - - - - -

Arnie [Palmer], usually a great putter, seems to be having trouble with his long putt. However he has no trouble dropping his shorts.

—*Broadcast commentator during a tournament*

Bailed Bonds

The baseball strike affected fans, owners, and players alike. It hit the fans emotionally, and it hit the owners and players financially. When the strike was in full force, San Francisco Giants outfielder Barry Bonds appeared before a San Francisco judge and requested that his child-support and alimony payments be cut in half. Bonds explained that when he was playing ball, he pulled in $4.75 million a year and paid out $15,000 a month in child support and alimony. But the strike put an end to his career highs, and now he was near the poverty level. The judge approved Bond's request, cut his payments in half, and then shocked the court by asking for Bond's autograph.

His reputation preceded him before he got here.

—*Don Mattingly, New York Yankee, on Mets pitcher Dwight Gooden*

Hey, Idiot!

Give Me a Break

In 1978, Jack Tatum of the Oakland Raiders made a "clothes-line" hit on New England Patriots receiver Darryl Stingley. The hit broke Stingley's neck and caused permanent paralysis. Not only didn't Tatum apologize for his maneuver, he claimed it was a legal hit and warned other opponents that they could expect the same. Nearly twenty years later in January 1997, Tatum applied to the NFL Players Association for disability benefits of $156,000. Tatum claimed that living with the fact that he had paralyzed someone had caused him mental anguish. How did he come up with the $156,000 fee? In the NFLPA it is the highest category for compensation—the "catastrophic injury" category. Ironically, it's the same category that Stingley, the man who was paralyzed, is in.

GATORS TO FACE SEMINOLES WITH PETERS OUT

—*Headline from the* Tallahassee Bugle

Hey, Idiot!

Dropping Your Guard

It's a play you won't find in any playbook. During a high school basketball game between Wadsworth and Copley High School in Ohio, a unique strategy was used to help maintain Copley's two-point lead. As a Wadsworth player prepared to throw an inbounds pass, a sixteen-year-old Copley student dove out of the stands and pulled down the player's shorts. The maneuver must have accomplished its goal, as Copley went on to win the game 65 to 60. The unidentified student was arrested as he tried to escape from the gymnasium. He was charged with disrupting a lawful meeting and disorderly conduct, both misdemeanors. The boy not only exposed his school's opponent, he also exposed himself to an unspecified number of days in suspension and was banned, thanks to Principal Bill Steffan, from extracurricular activities. I wonder if the boy thought he was doing a legitimate play—a drop shot, perhaps?

Officials, acting on a Major League Baseball policy permitting fans to wave only **"baseball related"** banners, confiscated the Reverend Guy Aubrey's **"John 3:16"** banner. Later the preacher returned with another banner that claimed, **"Go Reds—John 3:16."**

Foot Brawl

We've all heard of the Scottish soccer hooligans—rough fans of the sport known to wreak havoc before, during, and after a game—but who is the roughest element in the sport? How about the referees? That's right. A South African football referee was charged with murder after he shot dead a player who disagreed with him about a goal. Referee Petrus Mokgethi claimed he was acting in self-defense as the player, Isaac Mkhwetha, lunged at him with a knife after the opposing team scored a goal. The game was held in the gold mining town of Hartbeesfontein, 110 miles west of Johannesburg. I'll bet it made the half-time festivities pale in comparison.

My sister's expecting a baby, and I don't know if I'm going to be an uncle or an aunt.

—*Chuck Nevitt, North Carolina State University basketball player, as reported in* Sports Illustrated

Frozen Gas

Quinnipiac was leading Fairfield 2 to 1 at the Wonderland of Ice arena in Bridgeport, Connecticut, and fans and players alike started getting pretty sick about the whole thing. It wasn't the score that was turning everyone's stomach, it was the Zamboni machine. Apparently, an employee forgot to turn on the arena's exhaust fans when the ice-polishing machine entered the rink. Carbon monoxide fumes sent fourteen players to the hospital and canceled the game for the rest of the evening. I wonder if that's where the expression "You stink on ice" came from?

— — — — — — — — — —

People think we make $3 million and $4 million a year. They don't realize that most of us only make $500,000.

—*Pete Incaviglia of the Texas Rangers*

A Labor-Intensive Sport

One pregnant woman from Detroit, Michigan, showed why her city is known as "Hockeytown" when she demanded to see Game 1 of the Stanley Cup finals even though she was going into labor. The woman began having contractions on her way to Joe Louis Arena, but told her husband to keep going as she was determined to see the game. As her beloved Detroit Red Wings labored in their match with the Washington Capitals, the mother-to-be labored to keep her labor in check. To celebrate Detroit's 2 to 1 victory, the woman had a six-pound, four-ounce daughter—three hours after the game ended. I wonder if they decided to name the child in honor of the sport—Zamboni, perhaps?

He treats us like men.
He lets us wear earrings.

—*Torrin Polk, University of Houston receiver, on his coach
John Jenkins*

If You Say It They Will Listen

A Pittsburgh Pirates broadcaster broke into coverage of a Giants-Pirates baseball game to report that actor James Earl Jones had died. "A lot of us in baseball have a lot of feelings about *Field of Dreams* and the soliloquy he gave in it," announcer Larry Frattare lamented. A few minutes later, Frattare got back on the microphone with an update on the actor's condition—he's fine, he's not dead. The announcer had misunderstood his producer, who'd tried to tell him that the accused murderer of the Reverend Martin Luther King, Jr., James Earl Ray, had actually died. "I don't feel glad about it. In fact, I felt like a real fool," Frattare said. James Earl Jones was quite relieved to hear that he wasn't dead.

I'm not allowed to comment
on lousy no good officiating.

*—New Orleans Saints General Manager Jim Finks, when asked
what he thought of the referees after a loss*

Hey, Idiot!

Bet You Can't Do That Again!

At least eight golfers witnessed the most miraculous tee shot in golf history and have verified its authenticity. Todd Obuchowski got too much club behind his tee shot on the fourth hole at the Beaver Brook Golf Court in Lawrenceville, Massachusetts. The ball careered over the green of the 116-yard par 3 and onto a highway, hitting the passenger side of a passing Toyota driven by Nancy Bachand, ricocheted back to the green, and rolled into the cup for a hole-in-one. Everyone was happy for the thirty-four-year-old metal worker except the driver of the Toyota—her car suffered $150 in damages.

- - - - - - - - - -

```
        I think that the team that
  wins game five will win the series.
  Unless we lose game five.
```

—Charles Barkley

Legal
Idiots

Hey, Idiot!

Do You Swear to Tell the Truth, the Whole Truth...?

Robert B. Bowling a partner in the firm of Stumbo, Bowling, and Barber in Middlesboro, Kentucky, was questioning the wife of a man accused of resisting arrest and running from the police. Bowling was trying to prove the police had used excessive force and the defendant had escaped in order to protect himself. Bowling's exchange with the defendant's wife went like this:

Bowling: Do you believe the police officers were abusive or rough with your husband?

Witness: Yeah, they were slinging him around so he broke and run.

Bowling: What happened next?

Witness: The policeman asked me [my husband's] name and I told him I didn't know.

Bowling: What happened after that?

Witness: The police called me a fat, lying whore.

Bowling: What did you say to that?

Witness: I told him I ain't no liar.

No comment!

Hey, Idiot!

Puppy Love

A Montrose, Iowa, native filed a $30 lawsuit against her neighbor, claiming the man's beagle, Murphy, tore a hole in her screen door and impregnated her little Scottish terrier. The woman sought damages for the cost of an abortion. "She came up here asking me to pay for an abortion," said the beagle's owner about the complaint. "I told her I didn't think Murphy was the father. If he is the father, I think we should have some say on whether she should have had an abortion without consulting Murphy or myself. I'm opposed to abortion." Just like any relationship—the in-laws always get in the middle of things.

In Riverside, California, **no one is allowed** to carry a lunch pail or a lunch box on any street within the town's limits.

Hey, Idiot!

Eight Days a Week

A bankruptcy lawyer from Raleigh, North Carolina, was indicted on federal fraud charges because he billed clients an average of 1,200 hours a month. Why would anyone prosecute an attorney for slaving away 1,200 hours a month? Because a thirty-one-day month only has 744 hours. I've heard of working overtime, but it's about time this guy clocked out.

Louisville judge Edmond Karem decided the jury went **"a little bit far"** in recommending a 5,005-year sentence for a convicted robber and kidnapper. He gave the man a break and reduced the sentence to 1,001 years. With good behavior the guy could be out in 750 years.

Hey, Idiot!

Sick of the System

A man arrested on insurance fraud in Los Angeles filed a lawsuit against Equitable Life Assurance Society two years later, claiming that since the time of his arrest, he has suffered an allergic reaction to courthouses and, as a result, had been unable to continue work at his profession—as a lawyer. The lawyer stated that exposure to courtrooms and other aspects of the criminal justice system caused him stress, mood swings, and physical sickness. Equitable Life Assurance Society paid him $85,000 as a disability payment. Wait a minute; I thought it was called the criminal justice system?

A man charged with shooting his landlord was apprehended after skipping two court hearings in a Brooklyn, New York, courtroom. But a judge ordered the man to be released after he claimed the state had deprived him of his right to a speedy trial because it didn't try hard enough to catch him.

Hey, Idiot!

Rubbing the Judge the Wrong Way

In a twist of events, a lawyer was ruled to be "in contempt of court" by a judge because he had missed a court date. During his hearing on the charges, the lawyer explained that he "had the screaming itches of the crotch. I wasn't here because I would have been scratching my testicles constantly." The judge was aghast at what he termed a "degrading" explanation and ruled that the lawyer's fine be doubled. Finally, justice is served.

Even if you are visiting or simply passing through Lexington, Kentucky, it is **strictly forbidden** to carry an ice-cream cone in your back pocket.

Flower Power of Attorney

An angry attorney filed a lawsuit against the owner of a flower shop in Tarzana, California, accusing him of "malicious negligence." The lawyer claims he purchased a bouquet of flowers for his wife, who had just given birth to their daughter, and composed a love note to accompany the arrangement. The reason the lawyer sued was that the flower shop lost the note. The attorney refused to settle out of court, claiming the words he had written were unique and that "I'm a hard-nosed, aggressive plaintiff's attorney. [Composing the note was] one of the only times in my life that I was really inspired." I'm sure the flower shop had a few "unique" words for the lawyer, too.

An Arizona woman filed for damages and **received $356,250 for injuries she suffered** while in a Tucson court-room. The woman, who was serving as a juror at the time, hurt herself when she accidentally fell out of the jury box.

Hey, Idiot!

Brief Cases

- A Kansas City, Missouri, land developer filed a lawsuit against a former city councilman for the return of the $25,000 bribe he'd paid the councilman (even though they were both in prison at the time).

- In Knoxville, Tennessee, a woman sued a local McDonald's restaurant, claiming that an overly hot pickle fell out of the hamburger she was eating and badly burned her chin. She sued for $110,000 and her husband sued for $15,000, claiming loss of her services and consortium. But honestly, what kind of services and consortium did he lose if she can't even keep a pickle in her mouth?

- A woman sued the manufacturer of "The Clapper," which activates electronic appliances at the sound of a clap, claiming the product was defective and that she had to clap so hard to get it to work she "couldn't peel potatoes . . . I was in pain." The judge rejected the woman's claims on the grounds that she simply didn't adjust the device's sensitivity controls.

- A disabled woman sued the Action Mobility store in Lake Worth, Florida, on the grounds that it didn't have designated handicapped parking spaces. The store sells and services wheelchairs, and the disabled couple who owns the place insisted that nearly all their customers are handicapped.

Hey, Idiot!

Landing in the Rough

A recently widowed woman in Charleston, West Virginia, filed a lawsuit against the makers of a golf cart, claiming they had contributed to the untimely demise of her husband. He had been drinking heavily during a golf tournament, and he died when he fell out of the cart and struck his head. The bereaved wife claimed the company was negligent because the cart was designed without doors or seat belts. She is also suing her son, who was driving the cart at the time of the accident. Now, that would really tee you off, wouldn't it?

A Florida district appeals judge, caught shoplifting a VCR remote control, was ordered to be removed from the bench. The judge appealed the ruling, citing the Americans with Disabilities Act, on the grounds that he was **"depressed"** because his daughter didn't get into law school and his son was bringing home bad grades.

Laughing All the Way to the Bank

A woman who worked in a bank in Sikeston, Missouri, was accused and later found guilty of embezzling more than $168,000. Federal guidelines have established a minimum sentence for this crime of eighteen months in prison, unless, of course, you can prove "diminished capacity." Diminished capacity is a psychological phenomenon that causes the affected person to not know the difference between right and wrong. The woman's attorney claimed that his client suffered from this ailment because she was distraught over her inability to conceive a child. After hearing arguments from both sides, the judge ruled in favor of the woman and sentenced her to only four months in prison. Now, I'm not sure who has diminished capacity—the woman or the judge.

A group of men who competed in a foot race while carrying refrigerators on their backs sued the manufacturer because the appliances **carried insufficient warnings** of possible injury from such activity.

Hey, Idiot!

A Shocking Outcome

After drinking all night at a party in Chicago, a young man felt the call of nature and went to relieve himself, looking for an out-of-the-way place. The man, a foreigner who couldn't read English, staggered past signs reading DANGER, KEEP OUT, and ELECTRIC CURRENT. He stumbled and climbed over a row of uneven wooden boards laid on the ground as a means of deterring trespassers and wound up on the grounds of the Chicago Transit Authority's Ravenswood line. He proceeded to urinate on the third rail, which carries six hundred volts of electricity, and was electrocuted. The man's family, who figured out the English word for "sue," filed a lawsuit against the CTA for negligence and won. They were awarded $1.5 million. The CTA appealed the case, but it was upheld by the Illinois Supreme Court, which ruled that although the man was intoxicated and trespassing, and regardless of the warning signs and the barrier, the CTA was at fault and must fork over the cash. Thus transforming current to currency.

Trice v. Reynolds, et al.: Ex-chef sues because the food was bad, yet **he wanted bigger portions.**

Hey, Idiot!

Don't Bet on It

A man who should be spending his time in Gamblers Anonymous instead of the courtroom countersued the Sands Hotel Casino in Atlantic City, New Jersey, in retaliation for their suit against him. The casino sued the man in an attempt to recover the more than $1 million in credit they extended him so he could continue gambling at their casino. In turn, the gambler sued the hotel to have his debt canceled and have the casino pay all legal expenses as well as punitive damages for the way it treated him. The man claimed the casino treated him very well; he was personally escorted to his gaming tables and brought complimentary drinks by a waitress who waited on him exclusively. He complained that such wonderful treatment caused him to drink too much and that inevitably led to his great monetary losses, which he claimed he would have avoided easily otherwise. Yeah, I bet!

A psychic sued her doctor and was awarded $986,000 because she claimed the CAT scan she underwent had **suppressed her psychic powers** and severely affected her ability to make a living. Didn't she see that coming?

Hey, Idiot!

A Hand-Out Hand-Out

The Western Massachusetts Legal Services Corporation, a legal aid group, produced a brochure that explained how welfare recipients who received a financial windfall could still remain eligible for benefits. Usually, welfare recipients are not eligible for aid when they have more than $1,000 on hand. But the brochure explains that to get around that point, welfare recipients should simply "spend the money as quickly as possible." The brochure even supplied an example: "Martha gets her [Aid to Families with Dependent Children] checks on the 1st and 15th of each month. She knows she will be getting a settlement about the 20th of October. Since she wants to do some special things with the money, she goes to her local welfare office on Sept. 30 and signs their form requesting that she will be taken off AFDC Oct. 1. When the settlement money arrives, she spends it according to her plans and has spent all but $1,000 of it by Oct. 31. She then goes back to her local welfare office on Nov. 1 and reapplies to AFDC." If you can't beat the system, at least kick the crap out of it.

In Pennsylvania, it is **against the law to shoot bullfrogs** on Sunday.

Hey, Idiot!

One Beer Shy of a Six-Pack

A beer-loving man sued Anheuser-Busch for $100,000, claiming false advertising and failure to deliver on its promise. The man stated that regardless of how much Bud Light he drank, bikini-clad woman showering affection on him never material-ized like the commercials implied. To top it off, he claimed that drinking beer sometimes made him sick. He sued for "emotional distress" brought on by Anheuser-Busch's failure to provide "unrestricted merriment." The court ruled that no matter how much beer he'd had, he still didn't have a case.

In order to extend the reach of his ladder while working on his barn, a Pennsylvania man placed it on a pile of frozen horse manure. While he was working, the manure thawed enough to cause the ladder to slip, and the man fell and injured himself. He sued the manufacturer of the ladder, and a jury awarded him $330,000. **And that's no sh-t.**

Coin-Operated Justice

Try as they might, the jury of seven women and five men of the Jefferson County Circuit Court could not come to a decision in the trial of murder suspect Phillip J. Givens II. Since the thought of coming to a unanimous decision had been tossed aside, they decided to toss something else to make their decision—a silver dollar. "I didn't think we had anything to lose," said the foreman about the way the jury flipped off their responsibilities by flipping a coin. Shortly before sentencing, the judge discovered how the jury had reached its verdict and declared a mistrial. The judge said he had to call a mistrial because of the jury's mistake—in other words, he called it in the err.

A Florida man filed a lawsuit stemming from a haircut that he claimed was so bad that it induced a panic-anxiety attack and interfered with his **"right to enjoy life."**

Hey, Idiot!

Abusing the System

The lawyer of a man on trial for armed robbery was making a last-minute plea to the court before her client's sentencing. She was trying to explain to the court the man's erratic behavior and pointed out that his addiction to drugs drove him to robbery. The lawyer told the court that her client was a heroin user, and the drugs had clouded his reasoning. Several months after the trial the client sued his lawyer because, as stated in the lawsuit, she claimed he was a heroin user when, in fact, he was merely a cocaine addict. The man stated that hearing himself referred to as a heroin addict had given him post-traumatic stress disorder, resulting in lessened "self-confidence, self-esteem, and self-image." I guess being a cocaine user, the man thought he would take a crack at it.

A woman from North Dakota who was injured when her smoke detector failed to sound sued the manufacturer of the alarm. **The case was dismissed** when it was discovered the woman had failed to put batteries in the detector.

Judging a Judge

A California judicial board fact-finding panel concluded that a Los Angeles County judge was not entitled to the four hundred days' sick leave he had taken. The judge said that he had been plagued with various ailments, including a phobia for the job of judging, which contributed to his leaving the country and enrolling as a full-time medical student in Dominica while still collecting his $130,000 annual judicial salary. His court was really adjourned, wasn't it?

A woman filed a lawsuit in Halifax, Nova Scotia, asking about $7 million from Coca-Cola. She claims that while she was pregnant, a Fruitopia bottle shattered while she was drinking from it, slicing her lip and causing her to bite on slivers of glass. **But that's not why she's suing.** The woman claimed that the harrowing experience resulted in a fear of miscarriage that caused the fetus, now a child of three, to fail to trust and like her sufficiently.

Hey, Idiot!

Critter Catalog

The local Humane Society in Roy, Washington, knocked on the door of a residence, checking for licensing violations. They asked the seven-year-old boy to list the names of the pets that lived in the house and the boy mentioned several, including their cat, Patches. The Humane Society had no record of Patches having received a license, reported the little boy's mother to be in violation, and sent her a citation. The woman tried fighting the violation, but had no luck with the Humane Society. Eventually she took her claim all the way to a state judge, who ruled in her favor on the grounds that Patches, although a cat, was in fact a stuffed toy.

California requires a warning label on all packages that contain lead. This holds true for bullets (which contain lead). The warning reads: **"This product contains lead and may be hazardous to your health."**

Hey, Idiot!

More Brief Cases

- A Connecticut woman filed a $60 million lawsuit against Bridgestone/Firestone and Ford because for two months she lived in fear of imminent tire failure, regardless of the fact that no problem actually occurred with her tires.

- A convicted kidnapper serving forty-five years in a Maryland prison sued a typewriter company for $29,000 on the grounds that he would have won parole had his type-writer ribbon not broken while he worked on his brief.

- An Ohio man who won an All You Can Drink Contest sued the owners of the bar who ran the contest because he was so drunk that he fell down, hit his head, and was hospitalized. The man, who voluntarily entered the contest, and wound up with a blood alcohol level of .31 percent, is suing for $1 million.

- A left-handed postal clerk filed suit against the Postal Service, citing discriminatory bias in setting up filing cases primarily "for the convenience of right-handed clerks."

- The Sons of God Motorcycle Club Ministry won its federal trademark infringement suit against the Chosen Sons of God Motorcycle Club Ministries.

Hey, Idiot!

Crazy Is as Crazy Does

An unidentified Philadelphia man was denied a gun-carry permit by the Philadelphia Department of Licenses and Inspections. The man pleaded with the department panel that he needed the gun to protect himself from "dwarf drug dealers" who were "beaming radio waves" into him by satellite and thereby reading his mind. Earlier, the man's permit had been revoked when he'd showed up at a local hospital wrapped in aluminum foil and complaining about the pain caused by the radio waves, "There's been no evidence adduced before this panel that [my client] in any way is not of sound mind." Sounds like someone else has been the victim of radio waves, doesn't it?

Police shot and wounded one robber of a bar in Hayward, California, prompting the other three gunmen to go back into the bar and take hostages. One of the hostages got the drop on a robber, stabbing and killing him with a knife. The family of the deceased robber later sued the bar, claiming it failed to provide a **"safe environment"** for him.

"E" for Effort

A Pennsylvania woman sued her school and her professor because she failed a course and was therefore denied a diploma. The woman's lawsuit claims that she invested "time, effort, dedication, and money" in her studies at Edinboro University in Edinboro, Pennsylvania, in exchange for a degree from the college. But the school "rescinded and repudiated said agreement by issuing a grade of 'F' in clinical nursing without justification, cause, or merit." The woman's lawyer claims her client is unemployable without the degree and is seeking up to $20,000 or "reevaluation" of her clinical abilities and a nursing degree. A spokesman for the university stated that the woman was given a chance to take the test over, but her lawyer said that since her client is a single mother of two children, retaking the test wouldn't be possible.

Young v. Murphy: A Mississippi prisoner sued on the grounds that he didn't attend a scheduled parole hearing, even though **he had escaped from prison** and wasn't there when the hearing took place.

Hey, Idiot!

Blue Moon

As a prank, a University of Idaho student climbed on a three-foot-high heater in front of a third-floor dormitory window, dropped his pants and underwear, and pressed his bare bottom against the window, mooning his friends below. He lost his balance, however, and crashed though the window, winding up with four fractured vertebrae, abrasions to his hands, and "deeply bruised buttocks." After he picked himself up off the concrete, the embarrassed and injured student claimed, "This is just a freak accident." But a short six months later, he decided to sue the school for negligence in failing to warn dorm residents of "the danger associated with upper-story windows." He asked for $940,000 in damages—that's $470,000 per cheek, in case you were wondering. The claim was denied. "We've got a kid that's presumably of average intelligence with his bare bottom against a window, leaning back," said Al Campbell, claims manager for the state's Bureau of Risk Management. "That doesn't seem very bright to me."

The San Francisco Giants were sued for giving away **Father's Day gifts** to men only.

Unexplainable Idiots

Juiced and Juiced

Enraged that the electric company had the nerve to cut his power simply because he hadn't paid his bill, a Centerton, Arizona, man drank "four or five" beers and took matters into his own hands. He propped an aluminum ladder against a utility pole and climbed to the top. Using his bare hands, the man tried to reconnect the main power line and received a 7,620-volt shock. Amazingly, the only injuries he suffered were severe burns to his hands. I'm not sure why he needed the power turned on—it sounds to me like he was already well lit.

The zoo in Memphis, Tennessee, agreed to refund admission charges to several visitors to their special exhibit on dinosaurs. The people in question had complained to zoo officials after **they were shocked to discover** that the exhibit included no live dinosaurs.

Sit on It!

The Seattle, Washington, Police Department required the twenty-six employees in its fingerprint unit to attend a half-hour mandatory training session on how to sit in a chair. The safety class evolved after three employees filed workers' compensation claims for injuries they sustained after they hurt themselves attempting to sit in chairs with rollers. "Some people know how to sit in a chair," said department safety officer Patrick Sweeney, "while others need some instruction." The proper technique, according to an internal memo, is "Take hold of the arms and get control of the chair before sitting down."

A recently enacted Washington state law (SB 6161) requires that material released from the rear end of a cow henceforth be referred to as **"daily nutrients"** rather than **"manure."** However, the law is just cow hockey because it contains no penalty for failure to comply.

Body of Evidence

A funeral home worker from Columbus, Ohio, looking for some lively entertainment parked his hearse at a local strip joint called the Candy Store. Police noticed the hearse and decided to check it out. They were soon looking for the funeral home worker to let him know he had left something in the back—a dead body. The corpse was uncovered, "in plain view of anyone who walked by," said the local sheriff. The hearse driver was supposed to be transporting the body from northeastern Ohio to a funeral home 165 miles away. He pleaded innocent to charges of "abuse of a corpse," and if found guilty will face a stiff fine.

For some reason the Oregon Department of Environmental Quality expressed concern that Yamhill County Public Works **employees might choose to eat contaminated dirt.** In response, Public Works Director Bill Gille informed the DEQ that employees have been notified that the contaminated dirt is not edible.

Hey, Idiot!

Getting Your Goat

A farmer in Chaguana, in central Trinidad, alerted police to a man who had just stolen goats and sheep from his property. The police soon gave chase and spotted the man driving a rental car with its headlights out. The man pulled the car over to the side of the road and bailed out. Police investigating the car found several goats that, for some reason, were dressed up in shirts, pants, and hats and were accompanying a sheep wearing a dress. Authorities believe the thief may have dressed up the animals trying to fool people into thinking they were human passengers. I would have loved to have heard someone yelling to the fully clothed goat, "Hey, fellow, why such a long face?"

A bank robber was arrested in Durham, North Carolina, after presenting a teller with a note demanding money and a finely detailed drawing of a gun. **The man didn't actually have a gun** and was therefore not charged with armed robbery.

Hey, Idiot!

Please Hang Up and Try Again

An obscene telephone caller who was obsessed with calling and tormenting women dozens of times a day was finally arrested after placing more than forty thousand obscene calls in a three-year period. The flying finger's failure came when one of the women whom he had called nearly every day for six months said she was busy and asked if he would leave his number so she could call him back—he did.

Police officers in Yakima, Washington, quickly responded when they heard a single gunshot and saw a man frantically removing his flaming sport coat. After helping the man and then questioning him, **he confessed that he had been smoking a pipe,** and had stuck it, still lit, into his coat pocket that also contained some rags and a rifle cartridge. The burning pipe set the rags on fire, and that, in turn, caused the cartridge to explode. The spent bullet was recovered more than half a block away.

It's in the Can

Seeking revenge on her estranged husband, an Englishwoman hired a twelve-year-old girl and a fourteen-year-old boy for about $5.00 each to beat someone up so she could frame her husband for the crime. So who did the woman choose as her victim? Herself. And the strategy almost worked, too. The woman was brutally beaten, and authorities convicted her husband, a prison manager, of assault, and ordered him to pay a fine. Unfortunately for our bitter battered bride, the two children confessed to the crime. They told police the woman had hired them to beat her in the face (just the face, mind you), which they did, using cans of beans.

In Clearwater, Florida, two **wildlife poachers received severe burns** when they tried to knock birds off a transformer carrying fifteen thousand volts—with a metal pole.

Déjà-vu Again

Police had set up a sting in order to crack down on the number of vehicle thieves plaguing the city of Beckley, West Virginia. They used unclaimed property as bait to catch the burglars, and catch a thief they did. The man was arrested and charged with one count of grand larceny. The irony of the case is that the property used as bait was actually the same property the thief had been arrested for stealing two years before. Well, if at first you don't succeed.

A recently hired dispatcher for the Bridgeport, Connecticut, Police Department **was arrested when he was logged into the computer** and immediately identified as being wanted on a bad check warrant.

Paging Basil Fawlty

The owner of the Lighthouse Motel in Lincolnville, Maine, has been issued a court order making it illegal for him to speak to his own guests. Apparently, the man had a tendency to yell and be abusive to the guests at his motel, telling them they couldn't look at the rooms before they rented them. If they decided to leave, prosecutors charged, he would stand in front of their cars so they couldn't drive away. There was "overwhelming evidence" said Kennebec County Superior Court Justice Donald H. Marden, that the owner behaved in a threatening and aggressive manner, and he was fined $15,000. In addition to the fine, the court ordered that although he was allowed to continue running the business, he "can't have anything to do with any person lodging or seeking lodging at the Lighthouse Motel," prosecuting attorneys told the press.

A twenty-year-old Israeli woman who is terrified of cockroaches **suffered chemical burns** after spraying pesticide into her mouth when a flying cockroach landed on her tongue.

Hey, Idiot!

Greecing His Wheels

A British NATO soldier who got separated from his convoy turned south on the main road in Thessaloníki, a northern port city in Greece, trying to get back to his troops. Unfortunately, his company was in Skopje, Macedonia's capital, which lies north of where the soldier was. The man got into his jeep and drove the length of mainland Greece, stopping the car for directions only after winding up in Athens. Several authorities, including the British embassy, helped the Scottish military policeman get turned around and guided him on his four-hundred-mile journey to his camp. Join the Army and see the world!

A truck driver in Brussels, Belgium, thought he was following his doctor's orders by purchasing a bag of nails. After a hearty dinner, the man opened the bag and **started eating the small nails** one at a time. The man's doctor had told him that a diet heavy in iron would boost his sex drive and the man thought the nails would do the trick fast. He was rushed to the hospital after the nails ruptured his stomach.

Chicken Little

While doing calculations on possible meteor strikes from fragments of Comet Lee, a computer programmer at the Kennedy Space Station got some horrible news—the meteors were on their way. The man left his work and was found two days later hiding in a cave in southeast Ohio with camping equipment, dried food, and sixteen guns. The man told authorities that they were fools not to hide, because "He very sincerely thought there was a meteor that was going to hit the Atlantic Ocean and cause a tidal wave two hundred feet high," said police. "He was trying to hide from this meteor." Unfortunately, the programmer had entered some data wrong, and NASA stated that the closest Comet Lee will come to earth is 77 million miles. About how far out this fellow was from reality.

A Hiddenite, North Carolina, woman was arrested after police found a baby deer in the back of her four-wheel-drive vehicle. The deer was wearing cross-shaped, zircon-studded earrings about which the lady said, **"I thought it would be pretty."** The woman was arrested for cruelty to animals, fined $3,000, and faces up to a year in prison.

Hey, Idiot!

Personality Disorder

A man from Mexico, upon arriving at Oakland International Airport in California, was arrested for carrying faked U.S. documents. What's worse was that for some reason, the man had forged the documents using the identity of a fugitive wanted for felony burglary and carrying concealed weapons. "This guy basically cloned the identity of a wanted fugitive," a Customs Service spokesman said. "It seems like kind of a loser thing to do." The man was turned over to the U.S. Immigration and Naturalization service for questioning. The first question being, "What were you thinking?"

A San Francisco woman who didn't have a stove of her own stole the neighbors' gas stove without shutting off the gas first. **The apartment filled with gas and eventually exploded.** She was caught by Pacific Gas and Electric crews, who managed to stop the woman before she could cause another explosion—she had just connected the stove to her gas line with duct tape.

Put a Lid on It

A farmer from the northern province of Santiago del Estero, in Argentina, couldn't find a seat on the bus, so he climbed on top of the roof for the ride (not an uncommon practice in the country). The wind and cold were nearly unbearable, and the man crawled into a box strapped onto the roof rack. At the next stop, another man got up on the roof, since there still was no room inside the bus. As he was sitting there, the farmer inside the box, which, by the way, was a coffin, said, "Is it cold, sir?" The frightened man jumped off the moving bus and suffered a broken arm and leg.

Elgin, Ilinois, police report that their **"ride-along"** program—which allows citizens to accompany officers on patrol—has been successful in more ways than one. A detective thought he recognized Jason Miller, who showed up at a precinct station one night to take the tour, so he ran a computer check and found an outstanding warrant. Miller got his ride in a squad car—straight to the county jail.

Hey, Idiot!

Runaway Bride

While looking over the marriage announcement pages in her local newspaper, a London woman saw something she recognized. It wasn't a person—it was a dress. The woman identified the dress as having been stolen from her shop over four months ago. Since she had the full name of both the intended bride and the groom, the woman reported the incident to the police. "I was amazed that she had the cheek to let her picture be published in the paper wearing a dress stolen under my very nose," said the original dress's owner. The bride-to-be almost became a prisoner-to-be but was only fined $300 after she confessed to handling stolen property. If she'd been arrested, I wonder if the other prisoners would have chanted, "Here comes the bride. Here comes the bride."

A Marshfield, Wisconsin, man was unable to get money from an ATM machine so he decided to make a deposit instead. Security cameras caught the man as **he unzipped his pants** and urinated on the machine.

Hang Five to Ten

"**Y**ou'll never take me alive!" shouted the twenty-one-year-old man in a Santa Rosa, California, courtroom. The man climbed up on the defense table, jumped over to the court clerk's desk, then leapt threateningly to the judge's bench. Court deputies and two civilians tried to hold the man down as he flailed and fought with them. Eventually, he was shackled to a wheelchair and police rolled him off to jail. He was charged with resisting arrest, contempt of court, escape, threatening an executive officer, and battery on a police officer. What charges was the man in court for that day? Illegal skateboarding. Dude, you are so awesome!

A thirty-five-year-old man who had been dining in an Albuquerque restaurant pushed himself away from the table, went to the rest room, **climbed into the ceiling for some reason,** crawled around, and eventually fell through the kitchen ceiling. Even after questioning the man, police were unable to determine a motive.

A Couple of Doughnut Holes

After getting a call, an ambulance driver felt a little hungry. So he pulled his rig into the parking lot of a local doughnut shop in Houston, Texas, and went in for some pastries. The only problem with this scenario was that the driver was en route to the hospital during his unauthorized stop—with the patient waiting in the back of the ambulance. The driver, with a now "glazed" look in his eye, was arrested. The Houston Fire Department was put on a one-year probation and required to hire someone to supervise driver certification or pay a $33,000 fine. The fine obviously didn't have much effect; the next month the department was in trouble again for giving the former mayor a ride to the hospital in an unlicensed vehicle. You know, stopping for doughnuts or giving an illegal ride to the mayor is like six of one/half dozen of another.

One man wound up in the hospital and another landed in jail when they got into a fight over which one had the **hairiest butt.**

Hey, Idiot!

Up in Smoke

"If there was a charge for ignorance, this would be appropriate," said a prosecutor in Muskegon, Michigan. He was referring to the actions of a forty-year-old man who had been sitting in his bedroom sniffing propane gas from a twenty-pound cylinder. The man wanted to take his propane high to a higher level when he pulled out a joint, but he got higher than he could imagine after his house exploded when the flame from the cigarette lighter touched off the propane tank. The resulting explosion blew up part of the man's house and caused a fire that destroyed the building and damaged two neighboring houses. He could receive a jail sentence of up to twenty years for "unlawful possession or use of a harmful device causing property damage." Obviously the real damage occurred in this man's head a long time before the accident.

Two men were arrested for selling marijuana from a neighborhood ice-cream truck in Brooklyn, New York, after **drawing the attention of police** because the only customers in line were adults.

Hey, Idiot!

Trading Spaces

Police were dumbfounded at their actions but proceeded to arrest a couple who were living in an unoccupied (but not abandoned) house in Tunbridge, Vermont. The couple had begun an elaborate remodeling job on the home, laboring under the illusion that property should be shared rather than privately owned. The man and woman had removed some walls, reworked the plumbing, and were about to redo the bathroom when they were caught. They'd made money for their expensive renovation by selling antiques that were in the house. Although the owners liked what the couple had done with the place, they still had them arrested for criminal trespass and property damage. Said the arresting officer, "[They are] definitely [people] with a different mind-set." Ain't that the truth!

One half of a set of Siamese twins was so angered at his other half that he pulled out a loaded revolver and **shot his brother in the head.** Since they shared portions of the same circulatory system, they both died.

They Said What?

Unexplainable celebrity quotes.

- Alicia Silverstone: "I think that [the film] *Clueless* was very deep. I think it was deep in the way that it was very light. I think lightness has to come from a very deep place if it's true lightness."

- Richard Gere: "I know who I am. No one else knows who I am. If I was a giraffe and somebody said I was a snake, I'd think, 'No, actually I am a giraffe.'"

- At the 1994 Miss Universe contest, Miss Alabama was asked, "If you could live forever, would you and why?" Miss Alabama: "I would not live forever, because we should not live forever, because if we were supposed to live forever, then we would live forever, but we cannot live forever, which is why I would not live forever."

- Michael Jackson: "I have been the artist with the longest career, and I am so proud and honored to be chosen from heaven to be invincible."

- Singer Donny Osmond on returning to TV as host of the game show *Pyramid:* "I've been on TV ever since I was five," he said. "I'm forty-four now. I've been in the business forty years."

Hey, Idiot!

Take a Little off the Top

A sixty-three-year-old Fayetteville, North Carolina, woman was arrested for embezzling $1.1 million from the law firm where she worked and was sentenced to six years in prison. The law firm had hired her shortly after she had been convicted of embezzling from her previous employer. The attorneys knew the woman had been arrested for embezzling as they were the lawyers who defended her at her trial. I guess justice is blind sometimes.

———————————

A woman called with an unusual parking complaint. She said that she was upset because no one was parking in the handicapped space.

—*Verbatim excerpt from* City Talk, *the magazine published by Paramount, California*

Sandwich to Go, Please

A Dallas, Texas, police officer was fined $2,156 (in the form of lost wages) because he was caught eating on the job. The officer was suspended for fifteen days after he was caught eating a McDonald's chicken sandwich at the scene of an automobile accident. Why such a harsh sentence for simply eating on the job? Because the officer took the sandwich from the driver of the car involved in the accident. "You've got a broader issue than just the face value of the sandwich," said a police spokesman. "There are issues of ethics and the lack of compassion for a victim." I hope the officer didn't ask the car victim, "You get fries with this?"

A woman was arrested in Colombo, Sir Lanka, and charged with trying to pass a $1 million bill. To back up the scheme that the United States currency was real (by the way, there is no such thing as a $1 million bill), the woman supplied customers with a **"certificate of authenticity"** signed by officials of the International Association of Millionaires.

Hey, Idiot!

What a Crock!

While driving in Port Charlotte, Florida, a woman spotted an animal that had obviously been injured by a car. Feeling compassion for the beast, she gingerly picked it up off the road and carefully slid the animal into the backseat of her car. She decided that instead of calling the police or animal control she would take the injured creature home and nurse it back to health. The woman's neighbor warned the Good Samaritan that what she was doing was, in fact, illegal. Why? Because the woman had brought home an injured six-foot-long alligator. She panicked, hustled the alligator back into her car, and planned to release him in a nearby pond. But the animal, which might have been getting carsick by this time, thrashed around in the backseat so much that the woman crashed the car. "I knew I was in trouble, and I panicked and left," she said. "I had a felony in the backseat, and I just didn't know what to do." Police, however, knew just what to do—they arrested her and charged her with felony possession of an alligator, driving with a suspended license, leaving the scene of an accident, and resisting arrest. See ya later, alligator.

A San Diego man was arrested for allegedly assaulting his girlfriend in a supermarket parking lot with a **ten-pound tuna**.

Hey, Idiot!

I Don't Get It

Thinking he would get a good laugh at the expense of his wife, a Pennsylvania man poured tomato sauce on himself, fired his .22-caliber rifle in the house, and pretended he had been shot. The woman fell for the practical joke and called 911, pleading with them to send help for her wounded husband. When police arrived, they found the man very much alive, and since he was in possession of several guns, they also found him very much in violation of his parole. The man pleaded guilty to illegal ownership of firearms, and under the mandatory sentencing law for gun violations, he was sentenced to fifteen years to life. Turned out that the joke was on him.

The embarrassed South Gloucestershire council in the United Kingdom had to explain to residents that the opening of the new $2.5 million library would be postponed because **the council had forgotten to order any books.** Which really didn't matter too much, owing to the fact that they had also forgotten to budget for bookshelves.